W9-BXS-059

Also by Joel Osteen

Break Out!
I Declare
I Declare Personal Application Guide
Every Day a Friday
Every Day a Friday Journal
Daily Readings from Every Day a Friday
Your Best Life Now
Daily Readings from Your Best Life Now
Starting Your Best Life Now
Your Best Life Now Study Guide
Your Best Life Now for Moms
Your Best Life Begins Each Morning
Your Best Life Now Journal

BREAK
OUT!
Journ

BASED ON THE #1 *NEW YORK TIMES* BESTSELLER

BREAK OUT!

Journal

A Guide to Go Beyond Your Barriers
and Live an Extraordinary Life

JOEL OSTEEN

Faith
Words

New York • Boston • Nashville

Unless otherwise indicated, all Scripture quotations are taken from *The Holy Bible, New International Version*® NIV®. Copyright © 1973, 1978, 1984, 2011 by Biblica, Inc.™ Used by permission. All rights reserved worldwide.

Scripture quotations noted NLT are taken from the *Holy Bible*, New Living Translation, copyright © 1996, 2004, 2007 by Tyndale House Foundation. Used by permission of Tyndale House Publishers, Inc., Carol Stream, Illinois 60188. All rights reserved.

Scripture quotations noted NKJV are taken from the *New King James Version* of the Bible. Copyright © 1982 by Thomas Nelson, Inc. Used by permission. All rights reserved.

Scripture quotations noted AMP are from *The Amplified Bible*. Copyright © 1954, 1958, 1962, 1964, 1965, 1987 by The Lockman Foundation. All rights reserved. Used by permission. (www.Lockman.org)

Scripture quotations noted KJV are from the King James Version of the Holy Bible.

Literary development and design: Koechel Peterson & Associates, Inc., Minneapolis, Minnesota.

This book has been adapted from *Break Out*, copyright © 2013 by Joel Osteen. Published by FaithWords.

FaithWords
Hachette Book Group
237 Park Avenue New York, NY 10017
www.faithwords.com

Printed in the United States of America

First Edition: April 2014

10 9 8 7 6 5 4 3 2 1

FaithWords is a division of Hachette Book Group, Inc. The FaithWords name and logo are trademarks of Hachette Book Group, Inc.

The Hachette Speakers Bureau provides a wide range of authors for speaking events. To find out more, go to www.hachettespeakersbureau.com or call (866) 376-6591.

The publisher is not responsible for websites (or their content) that are not owned by the publisher.

Library of Congress Cataloging-in-Publication Data: 2013956774

ISBN: 978-1-4555-8262-4

Contents

Introduction

My book *Break Out! 5 Keys to Go Beyond Your Barriers and Live an Extraordinary Life* provides practical steps and encouragement for creating a life without limitations. When life weighs upon us, pushing us down, limiting our thinking, labeling us in negative ways, we have what it takes to overcome and rise above into the fullness of our destinies. Every person has seeds of greatness planted within by the Creator. When we break through in our minds, believing we can rise higher and overcome obstacles, then God will unleash the power within that will enable us to go beyond the ordinary into the extraordinary lives we were designed to live.

This journal companion for the book offers that same encouragement in daily doses supplemented by inspirational and thought-provoking material. Sometimes you need words of faith and victory spoken over your life. Words have created power. When you receive them into your spirit, they can ignite seeds of increase on the inside. That's the reason I've written this journal. You will find a wealth of Scriptures, inspirational quotations, selected stories, prayers, and points for contemplation. All are provided to engage you in a process of reflection that will enhance your faith and lead you to positive actions.

I am delighted in your interest in this book. It shows that you want to put action behind your faith and reach the highest level of your destiny, and God loves that. You'll learn five powerful keys for your life: to believe bigger, to consider God rather than circumstances, to pray God-sized prayers, to keep the right perspective, and to not settle for good enough.

My prayer is that you will take some time each day to read the entries and to add your own thoughts. But don't rush through it. Slow yourself down and take the time to reflect on your life. Let the Scriptures speak to your heart. If you are facing challenges or barriers, there are prayers and inspirational quotes to help remind you that God is with you each and every moment. Be still and listen to what God is saying through these words, then put words to your responses.

This is not a journal of daily events, but it's a journal to record life lessons that you don't want to forget. It's a reflection of your life journey. What you record you remember. You will discover that it will bring clarity to what God has done, is doing, and wants to do in your life.

Journaling has also been shown to improve problem-solving abilities. Many people find that using a journal helps them to better assess their thoughts and feelings and to find clarity. The process of putting pen to paper and then seeing your words on the page can help you solve problems while keeping matters in perspective and priorities straight. You may release pent-up emotions in the process, and that is a good thing, too.

Don't worry about punctuation, spelling, or grammar when making your own entries. You won't be graded on this. Simply let your thoughts and feelings flow.

This journal is designed to provide you twenty-five days of daily inspiration and encouragement in your walk of faith. It is best to read day to day in a quiet place where you can meditate and contemplate for brief periods, away from the usual distractions. Take your time and enter your own thoughts and encouragements. Once you've gone through it, feel free to begin again. Replenish your spirit and listen for the still, small voice of God's grace and direction.

Let this journal serve as a record of your daily progress and your entries as a testimony of your faith. Enjoy the process. Do your best, and you will go beyond your barriers and become everything God created you to be.

Part I:
Believe
Bigger

CHAPTER
1

Get Ready for a Shift

> **Key Truth**
> Our God has shifts in your future
> that will thrust you beyond barriers
> of the past into the extraordinary life
> you were designed to live.

Due to the recession, a construction manager I know had been out of a job for three years after twenty-five years of steady work at a successful company. He went to one job interview after another with no success, then finally took a much lower-level position in a small city, to which he had to travel a couple of hours every day. It was taking a toll on his health, his marriage, and his savings. It looked like his job situation would never change. But about six months later, his former boss called and said, "Hey, are you ready to go back to work?"

His old company had landed the largest contract in its history. He not only got his job back but also all of his benefits plus a significant salary increase and now he works locally. He said, "This is exceedingly, abundantly, above and beyond."

What happened? He came into a shift. Suddenly, things changed in his favor. One phone call. One contract. One good break. He went from barely getting by to having more than enough.

Zechariah said it this way: "'Not by might nor by power, but by my Spirit,' says the Lord Almighty" (Zechariah 4:6). That word *spirit* in the Hebrew means "breath." It's saying it will not happen just by your talent, just by your connections, just by those you know. It will happen because God breathes in our direction, shifts the winds, and blows healing and promotion, restoration, our way.

You were not created to just get by with an average, unrewarding, or unfulfilling life. God created you to leave your mark on this generation. You have gifts and talents that you have not tapped into. There are new levels of your destiny still in front of you. But *break out starts in your thinking.* As you put these keys into action, making room for increase, expecting shifts of God's favor, praying bold prayers, and keeping the right perspective, then God will release floods of His goodness that will thrust you beyond barriers of the past into the extraordinary life you were designed to live.

I'm declaring, "A shift is coming." A shift in your health, in your finances, or in a relationship. It may not look like it in the natural, but we serve a supernatural God. When He breathes in your direction, people change their mind. Closed doors suddenly open. The *no*s turn into *yes*es. *Not now* turns into *It's your time.*

The shift is acceleration. God's favor is being released in a new way that will propel you forward. He has shifts that will put you in positions you didn't earn, you didn't qualify for, or weren't next in line to receive. What should have taken you forty years to accomplish, God will do in a split second.

Why don't you start expecting unprecedented favor, believing for God to do something new in your life? Your attitude should be: "God, I'm ready. I'm taking the limits off of You. I'm enlarging my vision. I may not see a way, but I know You have a way. I declare I'm coming into a shift."

Consider This

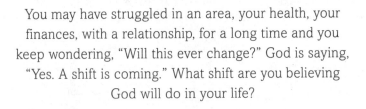

You may have struggled in an area, your health, your finances, with a relationship, for a long time and you keep wondering, "Will this ever change?" God is saying, "Yes. A shift is coming." What shift are you believing God will do in your life?

....
....
....
....
....
....
....
....
....
....
....
....
....
....
....
....
....
....
....

What the Scriptures Say

In the LORD's hand the king's heart is a stream of water
that he channels toward all who please him.

Proverbs 21:1

The LORD turned to [Gideon] and said, "Go in the strength you
have and save Israel out of Midian's hand. Am I not sending
you?" "Pardon me, my lord," Gideon replied, "but how can I
save Israel? My clan is the weakest in Manasseh, and I am the
least in my family." The LORD answered, "I will be with you . . ."

Judges 6:14–16

Thoughts for Today

—◈—

[Faith is] an inner conviction of being overwhelmed by God.

Gustof Aulén

He brought light out of darkness, not out of a lesser light, and He can bring your summer out of winter, though you have no spring. Though in the ways of fortune, understanding, or conscience you have been benighted until now, wintered and frozen, clouded and eclipsed, damped and benumbed, smothered and stupefied, now God comes to you, not as the dawning of the day, not as the bud of the spring, but as the sun at noon.

John Donne

Sorrow looks back. Worry looks around. Faith looks ahead.

Beatrice Fallon

....
....
....
....
....
....
....
....
....
....
....

A Prayer for Today

Father, thank You that You control the whole universe and nothing is too hard for You. I believe that You have given me gifts and talents that I have not tapped into and there are new levels of my destiny to which You are taking me. Thank You that You are breathing in my direction, shifting the winds of my life, and taking me where I could not have gone on my own. I expect to see Your hand of unprecedented favor working in ways exceedingly, abundantly, above and beyond my greatest dreams.

Takeaway Truth

God has shifts in your future that if He showed

you now you wouldn't believe. It's exceedingly,

abundantly, above and beyond. Suddenly, a dream

comes to pass. Suddenly, a promise is fulfilled. Suddenly,

the negative turns around. You need to get ready for

the surpassing greatness of God's favor!

CHAPTER
2
A Flood Is Coming

> ### *Key Truth*
> You are about to see a flood of God's goodness, a flood of opportunity, a flood of healing, a flood of good breaks, to where you are overwhelmed with His favor.

One time the Bible's King David needed a breakthrough. He faced an impossible situation. He and his men were up against this huge army—the Philistines. They were greatly outnumbered and had little or no chance of winning. David asked God for help, and God gave David the promise that He would go with them and they would defeat the opposing army, which was exactly what happened. David was so overwhelmed by the great victory, he said, "God has broken through my enemies by my hand like a breakthrough of water" (1 Chronicles 14:11 NKJV).

David named the place of his great victory Baal-Perazim, which means "the God of the breakthrough." Notice, David likened God's power to "a breakthrough" or "the bursting forth of water." In other words, he described it as a flood. He was saying that when the God of the breakthrough shows up and releases His power, it will be like a flood of His goodness, favor, healing, and new opportunities.

You may have difficulties that look extremely large, obstacles that look impassable, or dreams that look unattainable. But know this: When God releases a flood of His power, nothing will be able to stop you. That sickness may look big, but when God releases a flood of healing, it doesn't stand a chance. Your opposition may be stronger, better financed, better equipped, but when God opens up the floodgates, they'll be no match for you.

You may not have the connections to accomplish your dreams. You don't know the right people. You don't have the funding. But when God releases a flood of favor, people will come out of the woodwork to help you out. You won't have to look for them. Good breaks, opportunity, and the right people will all search you out.

You need to get ready, not for a trickle, not a stream, not a river, but a flood of God's favor, a tidal wave of God's goodness, a tsunami of His increase. God is going to take you to a level that you've never been before. It will be unprecedented. You will go farther and quicker than you ever dreamed.

Every one of us should have some Baal-Perazims. We should have places where we can look back and say, "That was where the God of the breakthrough did something amazing in my life. That was where God healed me. That was where God promoted me. That was where God protected me. That was where the God of the breakthrough visited my house."

What are you expecting? What are you believing for? Would you ever release your faith for something that big?

Dare to believe. If you think "trickle," you will receive a trickle. If you think "barely get by," then you will barely get by. If you think that your problem is too big, it will keep you defeated. But if you will learn to think "flood," you will experience a flood. If you think "overflow," you'll experience an overflow. If you dare think "tidal wave," then God can release a tidal wave of His goodness in your life. This is what Jesus said, "According to your faith it will be done unto you."

Consider This

---◇---

When you think of God's goodness toward you, what comes to mind? Do you think "trickle," "stream," or "flood"? What is keeping the God of the breakthrough from releasing a tidal wave of His power in your life that nothing can stop?

....
....
....
....
....
....
....
....
....
....
....
....
....
....
....
....
....
....

What the Scriptures Say

Then the LORD said: "I am making a covenant with you. Before all your people I will do wonders never before done in any nation in all the world. The people you live among will see how awesome is the work that I, the LORD, will do for you."

Exodus 34:10

I pray that your hearts will be flooded with light so that you can understand the confident hope he has given to those he called—his holy people who are his rich and glorious inheritance.

Ephesians 1:18 NLT

....

....

....

....

....

....

....

....

....

....

....

....

....

....

Thoughts for Today

However many blessings we expect from God, His infinite liberality will always exceed all our wishes and our thoughts.

John Calvin

God is always trying to give good things to us, but our hands are too full to receive them.

Augustine

I want to know God's thoughts. The rest are details.

Albert Einstein

....
....
....
....
....
....
....
....
....
....
....
....
....
....

A Prayer for Today

Father, this word is for me today. I'm raising my expectations. I'm shaking off doubt, negativity, disappointments, self-pity, little dreams, and little goals. I thank You that You want to do something new, something amazing in my life. You are God, the God of the breakthrough who has first place in my life. I believe that You are about to flood my life with Your goodness. I am believing You will open the windows of Heaven and pour out tidal waves of increase and joy and healing and mercy and blessings that cannot be stopped.

Takeaway Truth

You are under a Flash Flood Warning.

You're about to see the favor of God

profusely abound in your life. You are coming

into floods of healing, floods of wisdom,

floods of good breaks, floods of mercy.

Get ready for it. It's headed your way.

CHAPTER
3

Further Faster

> ### *Key Truth*
> Because you honor God,
> He will do in a fraction of the time
> what should have taken you a
> lifetime to accomplish.

In December 2003, we signed a sixty-year lease with the City of Houston for our Lakewood Church facility. Deep down I knew sometime during that sixty-year period God would give us the ability to purchase the building. In 2003, I was forty years old. I would be one hundred years old at the end of the lease. I prayed, "God, I want to purchase this building in my lifetime. I don't want to leave it up in the air for the next generation."

Seven years into our sixty-year lease, the city was running low on funds. They decided to sell off some of their excess properties to make up for the shortfall in the budget. The mayor's office called and asked if we would be interested in purchasing the facility, buying out the lease. A building like ours would cost $400 million to construct. Of course, we were interested, but we had to see what the sale price would be. The city did an appraisal, taking into account that any new buyer would still have to honor our sixty-year lease. The appraisal came back not at $100 million, not at $50 million, but at $7.5 million! Today, we own our beautiful facility free and clear.

Here's my point: What could have taken sixty years, God did fifty-three years sooner. He took us further faster. God has a faster calculator than we do, and He's speeding things up.

You may feel like you've fallen behind. Maybe you are not where you had hoped to be in life. You have big dreams in your heart, but you haven't caught any good breaks. Doors have closed. It's easy to get discouraged. But let me challenge you: If you will just keep being your best day in and day out, if you will live a life that honors God, He will not only make up for lost time, He also will thrust you further. He will do more than you can even ask or think.

Part of the shift is acceleration. It will not take as long to accomplish your goals as you think. It will not take as long to get out of that problem as it looks. Almighty God, the Creator of the universe, is breathing in your direction. He is causing things to fall into place. The right people will be drawn to you. Good breaks, opportunities, healing, restoration, favor. It's not business as usual. You've come into a shift. It will be business as unusual.

You don't know what God has already destined to come across your path. One phone call like we received, one contract, one good break, one inheritance, and you're totally debt free. You're into overflow. Now you need to get ready. God is saying, "It will happen sooner than you think. I am shifting things in your favor."

You will soon see acceleration. It will not take a lifetime to accomplish your dreams. It will happen in a fraction of the time. If you will take the limits off God, you will see Him do amazing things. Divine connections are coming your way. Like us, with the Lakewood Church building, what should have taken you sixty years will be accelerated to a few years. Because you honor God, He will take you further faster.

Consider This

---◆---

In His first public miracle, Jesus produced the finest-quality wine from water in a moment in time (John 2). Higher-quality wines take many years to make. What does that story tell you about what He can accomplish in your life? What acceleration are you believing God will do in your life?

....

....

....

....

....

....

....

....

....

....

....

....

....

....

....

....

....

....

....

....

What the Scriptures Say

His mother said to the servants, "Do whatever he tells you. . . ." Jesus said to the servants, "Fill the jars with water"; so they filled them to the brim. . . . and the master of the banquet tasted the water that had been turned into wine. He did not realize where it had come from, though the servants who had drawn the water knew. Then he called the bridegroom aside and said, "Everyone brings out the choice wine first and then the cheaper wine after the guests have had too much to drink; but you have saved the best till now."

John 2:5–10

And all these blessings shall come upon you and overtake you if you heed the voice of the Lord your God.

Deuteronomy 28:2 AMP

Thoughts for Today

The divine art of miracle is not an art of suspending
the pattern to which events conform, but of feeding
new events into that pattern.

C. S. Lewis

God's gifts put man's best dreams to shame.

Elizabeth Barrett Browning

We have forgotten the gracious Hand which preserved
us in peace and multiplied and enriched and strengthened us;
and we have vainly imagined, in the deceitfulness of our hearts,
that all these blessings were produced by some superior
wisdom and virtue of our own.

Abraham Lincoln

A Prayer for Today

Father in Heaven, I know You are the God of
Acceleration, and if You transformed water into wine
in a split second for the wedding party centuries ago, I
know You can accelerate things in my life. Thank You for
taking me further faster. I know You will thrust me years
ahead. I want to thank You that I will accomplish
my dreams sooner than I think.

Takeaway Truth

God is about to release everything that belongs to you. It will happen sooner than you think. It will be bigger than you imagined. He will bring out gifts and talents you didn't even know you had. He will open up new doors of opportunity. God loves to do exceedingly, abundantly, above and beyond.

CHAPTER
4

Explosive Blessings

Key Truth

God has explosive blessings coming your way—"sudden, widespread increase"—that you've never dreamed of.

I was driving through the mountains not long ago, and on one side there was a huge wall of rock where the road had been cut into the mountainside. The builders had used dynamite to blast away the rock; otherwise, the stone would have been there probably forever.

We all have things in our lives that seem permanent. Maybe it looks like you will never get out of debt, or like you will stay at the same earning level the rest of your life. But just as the builders used dynamite to blast away the rock so they could create that mountain road, God has explosive blessings that will remove obstacles, which may look permanent now. One touch of God's favor can blast you out of debt. One good break can blast you to a new level.

In 1946, Truett Cathy and his brother opened a little restaurant, the Dwarf Grill, south of downtown Atlanta. He noticed that hamburgers were the rage. But one day God gave him an idea. He thought if people like hamburgers, maybe they'd like chicken sandwiches, too. So he started to offer boneless chicken breast sandwiches to his customers, too. They were so popular, he opened his first shopping mall fast food restaurant in 1967 and called it Chick-fil-A. Today, there are more than 1,700 Chick-fil-As in thirty-nine states. The Cathys give millions of dollars to help people around the world—an explosive blessing.

You may think your current situation is permanent. You've been there a long time, and you can't see how you could ever move up. All the facts are telling you it's impossible that things will improve, but God has ways to increase you that you've never dreamed of. He's saying today: "You need to get ready. I have explosive blessings coming your way. I will take you higher. I will increase you beyond your income. I will suddenly change things for the better in your life."

One definition of the word *explosion* is "a sudden, widespread increase." That's what God will do for you. Suddenly, you're not expecting anything. It's out of the ordinary. It's not small. It's not mediocre. It's a widespread increase. It's so amazing you'll know it's the hand of God.

I've learned God doesn't always take us ahead in normal increments. There are times where God takes us little by little. We have to be faithful day in and day out, but when you hit an explosive blessing instead of moving up from seven to eight you'll go from seven to thirty-four. That's widespread increase.

This is the generation for the surpassing greatness of God's favor. The economy in Heaven is doing just fine. As long as we stay connected to the vine, putting our trust in Him, then you and I are connected to a supply line that will never run dry. Release your faith for explosive blessings. Believe that you can break out of what's holding you back and become everything God created you to be. Incredible power is released when we believe.

Consider This

—◇—

The psalmist David said, "What would have happened to
me if I would not have believed I would see the goodness
of God?" He learned to live in the surpassing greatness
of God's favor. Can you describe what that looks like?
How might God bring explosive blessings across your
path that are greater than you can imagine?

. . . .

. . . .

. . . .

. . . .

. . . .

. . . .

. . . .

. . . .

. . . .

. . . .

. . . .

. . . .

. . . .

. . . .

. . . .

What the Scriptures Say

"The poor and needy search for water, but there is none; their tongues are parched with thirst. But I the LORD will answer them; I, the God of Israel, will not forsake them. I will make rivers flow on barren heights, and springs within the valleys. I will turn the desert into pools of water, and the parched ground into springs."

Isaiah 41:17–18

"I will give you hidden treasures, riches stored in secret places, so that you may know that I am the LORD, the God of Israel, who summons you by name."

Isaiah 45:3

Thoughts for Today

Many Christians estimate difficulties in the light of their own resources, and thus attempt little and often fail in the little they attempt. All God's giants have been weak men who did great things for God because they reckoned on His power and presence with them.

Hudson Taylor

God has great things in store for His people;
they ought to have large expectations.

C. H. Spurgeon

God has in Himself all power to defend you, all wisdom to direct you, all mercy to pardon you, all grace to enrich you, all righteousness to clothe you, all goodness to supply you, and all happiness to crown you.

Thomas Brooks

A Prayer for Today

Father God, I may not see how it can happen, but I know You have explosive blessings coming my way. Thank You that You make rivers in the desert and streams in barren places. I'm expecting a sudden, widespread increase. I'm expecting to rise to a new level. I believe that I will see the surpassing greatness of Your favor and blessings that will catapult me years ahead. My hopes and dreams are in Your hands. I trust You.

Takeaway Truth

Where you are is not permanent. God has

explosive blessings in your future. Blessings

that will blast you to a new level. Immeasur-

able, limitless, surpassing favor is coming that

will take you beyond previous limitations.

CHAPTER
5

Increase Your Capacity to Receive

> ### Key Truth
> Enlarge your vision and make room for the new things God wants to do.

Even though God has amazing things in your future, He is limited by your capacity to receive. It's as if you have a one-gallon bucket, yet He has fifty gallons to give you. The problem is not with the supply but with your capacity to receive.

If you think you've reached your limits—whether it's because of a bad economy, your health is poor, or you can't afford the house you want—God has the ability and resources to help you, but your container is too small. You can't go around thinking thoughts of mediocrity and expect to excel. You can't think thoughts of lack and expect to have abundance. The two don't go together.

You have to enlarge your vision and make room for the new things God wants to do. If you trade in that small container and get something bigger, He can give you more. Your attitude should be: "The economy may be down, but I know God is still on the Throne. I know He has promotion and increase already lined up for me. His favor surrounds me like a shield. Goodness and mercy are following me. This will be a great year."

In 2 Kings 4 there's a story of a widow whose husband died. She doesn't have money to pay her bills. The creditors are coming to take her sons as payment. All she has of any value is a small pot of oil. Elisha the Prophet stops by her house and tells her to do something strange—to go to her neighbors and borrow as many big empty pots as she can find. These pots normally hold very expensive cooking oil.

He told her specifically, "Borrow not a few." He was saying, "Don't shortchange yourself. Make room for abundance." She went out and gathered as many empty pots as she could borrow. When she returned, Elisha told her to pour the little oil that she had into one of those empty containers. It looked as if she was just transferring it from one to another, but the Scripture says the oil never ran out. She kept pouring and pouring. God supernaturally multiplied that oil until every one of those containers was completely full.

Here's my point: She determined how much oil she would have to sell and pay off her debts. Whether she had one container, ten containers, or fifty containers, they would have been full.

My question is: How many containers are you borrowing? What kind of vision do you have for your life? God can do exceedingly abundantly above and beyond. He is El Shaddai, the God who is more than enough. You're making room for this far-and-beyond favor. You're positioned under the open windows of Heaven.

God is saying, "You need to get ready. I'm going to fill your containers." It may not have happened yet, but God has favor in your future. He has good breaks, opportunities, and blessings that will chase you down.

Make sure you don't shortchange yourself. God is saying to you what He said to this lady: "Borrow not a few." Don't limit your vision. You may not see how it could happen. That's okay; that's not your job. Your job is to believe. God has a thousand ways to fill your containers that you've never thought of.

Consider This

Psalm 81:10 says, "I am the LORD your God . . . Open wide your mouth and I will fill it." The question is: Do you have your mouth opened wide? Do you believe in increase? Do you go out each day knowing that favor is in your future? If you feel you are stuck in a rut, how do you get out of it?

What the Scriptures Say

When he had gone indoors, the blind men came to him,
and he asked them, "Do you believe that I am able to do
this?" "Yes, Lord," they replied. Then he touched their eyes
and said, "According to your faith let it be done to you";
and their sight was restored.

Matthew 9:28–30

Jabez cried out to the God of Israel, "Oh, that you would
bless me and enlarge my territory! Let your hand be
with me, and keep me from harm so that I will be free
from pain." And God granted his request.

1 Chronicles 4:10

Thoughts for Today

Whether you believe you can do a thing or not, you are right.

Henry Ford

There are no constraints on the human mind,
no walls around the human spirit, no barriers to our
progress except those we ourselves erect.

Ronald Reagan

Courage is a door that can only be opened from the inside.

Terry Neil

A Prayer for Today

Father, thank You that You are El Shaddai, the God who is more than enough. This is my year to go to a new level. This is my year to see a supernatural increase. I am making room for Your far-and-beyond favor. I am positioned under the open windows of Heaven with empty containers ready for You to fill. Do a new work in me, take me beyond the barriers of the past, and help me to step into the abundance You have in store.

Takeaway Truth

God has a barn load of blessings stored up for you.

Don't let a limited mind-set hold you back. You may not

see how it can happen, but God has a way. If you'll take

off the limits and make room for Him to do something

new, you'll go beyond the barriers of the past and step

into the abundance God has in store.

Part II:
Consider God, Not Circumstances

CHAPTER
6

Unshakable Faith

> ### *Key Truth*
> When God puts a promise in your heart, you have to come to the place where you believe in that promise so strongly no one and no circumstance can move you.

Knowing that extremely difficult circumstances awaited him, the Apostle Paul stated: "None of these things move me" (Acts 20:24 NKJV). His attitude was: "It doesn't change my mind. I'm not moved by what I see. I am moved by what I know. And I know if God is for me, who dares be against me? I know all of God's promises are yes and amen. I know God has the final say."

When God puts a promise in your heart, you have to come to the place where you believe in that promise so strongly no one can talk you out of it. It may seem impossible. Your medical report may say there's no way you will get well. It may look like you'll never get out of debt. All the circumstances may indicate you'll never accomplish your dreams, never meet the right person, or never see your family restored. But deep down you've got to have this unshakable confidence—a knowing that God is on the Throne working on your behalf, so you go out each day with passion, with expectancy, and looking for the great things God has in store.

Abraham did just that. God gave him a promise that his wife

would have a child. In the natural, childbirth was impossible for them. Abraham and his wife Sarah were each nearly a hundred years old. But it says, "Abraham never wavered in believing God's promise. In fact, his faith grew stronger, and in this he brought glory to God. He was fully convinced that God is able to do whatever he promises" (Romans 4:20–21 NLT). How could Abraham have this unwavering faith when in the natural all the odds were against him? I could see how he could have had at least a glimmer of hope, but it says he was fully convinced.

What was his secret? "He did not consider his own body . . . and the deadness of Sarah's womb" (Romans 4:19 NKJV). The key to having unshakable faith is to not consider your circumstances, but consider your God. Your circumstances, like Sarah's womb, may look barren. Your financial situation may look impossible. The medical report may look hopeless. All the experts may say you will never accomplish your dreams.

If you consider only the negatives, you will be discouraged and doubt will creep in, keeping you from God's best.

You must be like Abraham instead and say, "I will not focus on the negative things my mind or what the experts are telling me. I will not focus on how big my problems are. Instead, I will focus on how big my God is. He spoke the world into existence. He flung the stars into space. He's not limited by the natural. He has supernatural power."

When you focus on God instead of on your circumstances, doubt, fear, anxiety, and negativity don't have a chance. When you make God bigger, your problems become smaller. When you magnify God instead of magnifying your difficulties, faith rises in your heart. That faith will keep you fully persuaded that God will make a way, even though you don't see a way. And the beauty is that God will show up and do amazing things!

Consider This

You may be spending too much time analyzing your situation. You may have so many facts and figures that you've talked yourself out of what God can do. In the Scripture, God asks Abraham, "Is anything too hard for the Lord?" If you spent more time considering your God and thinking about His greatness and the times He's made a way in the past—dwelling on His promises, declaring victory and favor—what difference might it make in your life?

What the Scriptures Say

When he had finished speaking, he said to Simon,
"Put out into deep water, and let down the nets for a catch."
Simon answered, "Master, we've worked hard all night and
haven't caught anything. But because you say so, I will let down
the nets." When they had done so, they caught such a large
number of fish that their nets began to break.

Luke 5:4–6

Jesus looked at them and said, "With man this is impossible,
but with God all things are possible."

Matthew 19:26

Thoughts for Today

Abraham's unwavering faith arose from his great thoughts
of Him who had promised. He kept saying to himself, He is
able, He is able. He knew that God would not have said what
He could not perform. He knew that the God of nature was
Lord of the nature He had made. He knew that no word of the
Almighty was destitute of power. He fed his faith by cherishing
lofty and profound thoughts of God's infinite resources. There
rang in his heart the assurance, I am El Shaddai.

F. B. Meyer

The life of faith is not a life of mounting up with wings, but a
life of walking and not fainting. . . . Faith never knows where it
is being led, but it loves and knows the One who is leading."

Oswald Chambers

Faith does not operate in the realm of the possible.
There is no glory for God in that which is humanly possible.
Faith begins where man's power ends.

George Müller

A Prayer for Today

Father in Heaven, You are the Great I Am. You are
everything I need. If I am sick, You are my healer. If
I am struggling, You are my provider. If I am worried,
You are my peace. If I am lonely, You are my friend.
If I am in trouble, You are my deliverer. If I need a
break, You are my favor. I believe that what You have
spoken over my life You will bring to pass, and that
what You have promised You will do.

Takeaway Truth

It's time to start considering your God. He is the

all-powerful Creator of the universe. What He has

spoken over your life may seem impossible. It may

look too big. When you run the numbers, it may

not seem logical. Don't try to reason it out, because

you'll talk yourself out of it. Do as Abraham did

and become fully convinced.

CHAPTER 7

Be Confident in What You Have

> ### *Key Truth*
> You are equipped, empowered, and anointed by the Creator of the universe for all He has planned for you.

It's easy to focus on what we don't have. People tell me often that they don't have the talent, the education, or the personality they'd like to have, but as long as you think you're lacking, it will keep you from God's best. It's not enough to just have faith in God. That's important, but you should take it one step further and have faith in what God has given you. You have to believe you are equipped. You are empowered. You have the talent, the resources, the personality, everything you need to fulfill your destiny.

Here's the key: You don't need a lot of talent. You have exactly what you need. If you will use what God has given you, He will get you to where you're supposed to be. I've learned it's not necessarily the amount of talent, the amount of education, or the amount of money. What makes the difference is God's anointing on your life. You can have average talent, but when God breathes in your direction, you'll go further than someone with exceptional talent.

When my father went to be with the Lord in 1999, I knew I was supposed to step up and pastor the church, but I had never ministered before. I thought of all the reasons I couldn't do it. I don't have the experience. I don't have the training. I don't have the booming voice. I don't have the dynamic personality. On and on, I came up with all these excuses.

One day I heard God say something to me, not out loud, but just inside my heart. He said, "Joel, you've told Me all about what you don't have. I'm not interested in that. All I'm asking you to do is use what you do have." I stepped out with a little talent, a little ability, a little experience, and a little confidence. I didn't have much to give, but I realize now I had exactly what I needed. It looked small. It seemed ordinary.

God is a God of multiplication. When you give God what you have, He will take the little and He will turn it into much. Now quit telling God what you don't have and what you can't do. Be confident. You have exactly what you need. It may not be as much as others have, and that's okay. You're not running their race. Don't envy their talent. Don't covet what they have. Don't wish you had their looks, their personality, or their opportunities.

If God gave that to you, it wouldn't help you; it would hinder you. You're not anointed to be them; you're anointed to be you. When God breathed His life into you, He equipped you with everything you need to fulfill your destiny. You have the talent, the confidence, the strength, and the creativity to fulfill your purpose.

Now it may seem small at first. When I started, I felt unqualified and intimidated. But as you take steps of faith, believing that you are equipped, and confident in what God has given you, God will take the small and He will multiply it. One day you will look up and say, just as I did, "How in the world did I get to where I am?"

That's the goodness and favor of God.

Consider This

When David went to face Goliath, all he had was a slingshot and five smooth stones. It didn't look like much. But David understood this principle: Even though his slingshot was small, he realized it was given to him by God as part of his divine destiny. So what is it in your life that God has given you that He is breathing on and wanting to multiply?

What the Scriptures Say

[Jesus] replied, "You give [the crowd of about 5,000 men] something to eat." [The disciples] answered, "We have only five loaves of bread and two fish . . ." But he said to his disciples, "Have them sit down in groups of about fifty each. . . .Taking the five loaves and the two fish and looking up to heaven, he gave thanks and broke them. Then he gave them to the disciples to distribute to the people. They all ate and were satisfied, and the disciples picked up twelve basketfuls of broken pieces that were left over.

Luke 9:13–17

Moses answered, "What if they do not believe me or listen to me and say, 'The LORD did not appear to you'?" Then the LORD said to him, "What is that in your hand?" "A staff," he replied. The LORD said, "Throw it on the ground." Moses threw it on the ground and it became a snake, and he ran from it. Then the LORD said to him, "Reach out your hand and take it by the tail." So Moses reached out and took hold of the snake and it turned back into a staff in his hand. "This," said the LORD, "is so that they may believe that the LORD, the God of their fathers—the God of Abraham, the God of Isaac and the God of Jacob—has appeared to you."

Exodus 4:1–5

Thoughts for Today

I would rather be what God chose to make me than the most glorious creature that I could think of; for to have been thought about, born in God's thought, and then made by God, is the dearest, grandest, and most precious thing in all thinking.

George MacDonald

What have we to expect? Anything. What have we to hope for? Everything. What have we to fear? Nothing.

Edward B. Pusey

God has made me for a purpose—for China; but He has also made me fast, and when I run, I feel His pleasure.

Eric Liddell, Chariots of Fire

A Prayer for Today

———◆———

Father God, You are the most powerful force in the universe and You made me just the way I am. I don't know how all the situations in my life are going to work out. I don't know how my dreams can come to pass. But I trust You. My life is in Your hands. I believe that I am anointed, equipped, empowered, the right size, the right nationality, and the right personality. I know the right people. I have the right amount of talent. I believe that I have exactly what I need to fulfill my destiny. In Jesus' name, Amen.

....
....
....
....
....
....
....
....
....
....
....
....
....
....
....
....

Takeaway Truth

Right now God is breathing on your dreams.

He is going to multiply what you have. He

will multiply your talent, your resources, and

your creativity. This is not the time to shrink

back in fear. This is the time to move forward

in faith. Get up every morning knowing you

are anointed. You are equipped. You are

empowered. You have everything you

need to fulfill your destiny.

CHAPTER
8

Yes Is in Your Future

> ### Key Truth
> In His plan for your life, God already has your *yes*es planned out. The key is, you have to go through the *no*s to get to your *yes*es.

When God laid out the plan for your life, He lined up the right people, the right breaks, and the right opportunities. He already has your *yes*es planned out. Yes, to that promotion. Yes, to a clean bill of health. Yes, you will get married. Yes, you will be accepted into college. You may have been told *no* a thousand times, but God has the final say, and He says, "*Yes* is coming your way." *Yes*es are in your future.

Now here's the key: On the way to *yes* there will be *no*s. You have to go through the *no*s to get to your *yes*es. The mistake many people make is that they become discouraged by the *no*s and they quit trying. They worked hard but didn't get promoted. They prayed and believed but didn't qualify for the new home. They put time and energy into a relationship, but it didn't work out. Now they think it will never happen.

You have to go through your closed doors before you reach your open doors. When you come to a *no*, instead of being discouraged the correct attitude is "I'm one step closer to my *yes*."

What if you could see into your future and discovered you would receive twenty *no*s before you came to your *yes*? Then you'd be prepared to handle it when you faced a disappointment or a setback. You wouldn't give up if a loan didn't go through, or you didn't get a big sales contract you'd hoped to land. You would just check it off and say, "All right. Now I'm only nineteen away from my *yes*." Rather than being discouraged, you would be encouraged every time you heard a *no*.

But too many people, because they've hit several *no*s in a row, lose their passion. You've got to get this down in your spirit. *Yes* is in your future. You may have been turned down, delayed, overlooked. That was all a part of God's plan. The *no* is simply a test. Will you become discouraged and settle where you are? Or will you keep moving forward knowing that *yes*es are coming your way?

When Thomas Edison was trying to invent the lightbulb, he failed on his first two thousand attempts. Two thousand times he tried and it didn't work out. Two thousand times he was told *no*. He could have given up and quit, but he just kept looking for that one *yes*. After Edison came up with a working lightbulb, a reporter asked him about all of his failed experiments. He said, "I never failed once. I just found two thousand ways that wouldn't work."

God knows what He is doing in your life. You may be in a *no* right now. Maybe a relationship ended, or you were passed over for a promotion, or you lost a loved one. Don't be discouraged. Instead, say, "I may be in a *no*, but I'll never give up on my dream. I know a *yes* is coming. Favor is coming. Healing is coming. Promotion is coming. I will not become stuck in a *no*. I know *yes*es are in my future."

Consider This

❖

In 1 Kings 18, the Prophet Elijah went to the top of Mount Carmel and prayed and asked God to end the great drought. After praying, he said to the people, "I can hear the sound of an abundance of rain." He was saying, "There's a *yes* in our future. Rain is coming." Seven times Elijah told his assistant to look on the other side of the mountain to see if there was any sign of rain, and he got six *no*s before the desired *yes*. What does it mean to you that God has a *yes* in your future?

....
....
....
....
....
....
....
....
....
....
....
....
....
....
....
....

What the Scriptures Say

For all the promises of God in Him are Yes, and in Him Amen,
to the glory of God through us.

2 Corinthians 1:20 NKJV

Three times I pleaded with the Lord to take it
away from me. But he said to me, "My grace is sufficient
for you, for my power is made perfect in weakness." Therefore
I will boast all the more gladly about my weaknesses,
so that Christ's power may rest on me.

2 Corinthians 12:8–9

Thoughts for Today

If I had to select one quality, one personal characteristic
that I regard as being most highly correlated with success,
whatever the field, I would pick the trait of persistence.
Determination. The will to endure to the end, to get knocked
down seventy times and get up off the floor saying,
"Here comes number seventy-one!"

Richard DeVos

Inspiration without perspiration leads to
frustration and stagnation.

Bill Bright

Most people give up just when they're about to achieve success. They quit on the one-yard line. They give up at the last
minute of the game, one foot from a winning touchdown.

H. Ross Perot

....
....
....
....
....
....
....
....
....
....
....

A Prayer for Today

Father, thank You that You know what You are doing in my life. You put a dream in my heart, You've given me a promise on the inside, and deep down I know that I will succeed. There are *yes*es in my future, and by faith I am looking for them. I will keep looking to You, keep expecting, keep dreaming. My mind is made-up, and I am in it to win it. People will not talk me out of it. I will not give up because it doesn't happen on my timetable. I will not settle for second best because a few doors have closed. I believe that You will bring me through to my *yes*.

Takeaway Truth

Do not feel badly because you're not where you

want to be right this minute. Don't focus on the

disappointment, the failure, or the mistakes. They

were all a part of God's plan to prepare you for your

yes. Keep moving forward, being your best, honor-

ing God, being determined and persistent, and God

promises *yes* is in your future.

CHAPTER
9

God Is Preparing the Way for Victory

> ### *Key Truth*
> God is going before you to fight
> your battles and make your
> crooked places straight.

We all face situations that seem impossible. It's easy to become discouraged and think that things will never work out. But the Scripture says God is going before us making our crooked places straight. You may not have the connections right now to accomplish your dreams, but you don't have to worry. God is going before you and lining up the right people. He's arranging the right breaks, the right opportunities.

You may have lost a job or had your hours cut back. It's easy to get negative and think nothing will ever change. But you have to realize this loss is not a surprise to God. He's not up in the heavens scratching His head, thinking, "Oh, no. Now what will I do?"

God has already written every day of your life in His book. He knew exactly when that setback would occur, and the good news is He has already arranged a comeback. Before you had the problem, God already had the solution. He is going before you right now preparing the next chapter of your life. If you will stay in faith and keep the right attitude, you will enter a better chapter, a chapter with greater victories and greater fulfillment.

The Scripture tells us that the people of Israel faced an impossible situation. They stood by the Jordan River, about to cross over and go into the Promised Land. But this land was occupied by incredibly strong, powerful people called the Anakites, who were actually descendants of giants. In the natural, the people of Israel didn't have a chance. You can imagine how intimidated they must have felt knowing that they had to face these huge warriors. As they stood there at the Jordan, no doubt contemplating whether or not they should go through with it, God gave them a promise that helped push them over.

He said, "Today you are about to . . . take over the land belonging to nations much greater and more powerful than you. . . . You've heard the saying, 'Who can stand up to the Anakites?' But recognize today that the LORD your God is the one who will cross over ahead of you like a devouring fire to destroy them. He will subdue them so that you will quickly conquer . . ." (Deuteronomy 9:1–3 NLT).

You need to receive this word from God in your spirit. You will come out of trouble quicker than you think. God is fighting your battles for you. You will get well quicker than you think. Your recovery will amaze the doctors. You will accomplish your dreams much quicker than you think. Supernatural breaks are coming your way. How could this be? The Lord your God is crossing over ahead of you.

Switch over into faith. Get in agreement with God. Those obstacles trying to hold you back don't have a chance. Nothing can stand against our God. Turn around those negative thoughts that say you will never get well, never accomplish your dreams, or never overcome an addiction. You won't do this by your own strength or by your own power. You will accomplish this because Almighty God, the One who holds your future in His hands, will go before you, fighting your battles and making crooked places straight.

Consider This

—◇—

We all face modern-day Anakites. We hear the economy is down. A medical report comes back and tells us we're sick. Someone tells us we don't have what it takes. If you believe that God is going out before you, how should that influence your prayers and confidence as regards the giants you face? Is it making that impact on yours?

....

....

....

....

....

....

....

....

....

....

....

....

....

....

....

....

....

....

What the Scriptures Say

"The crooked roads shall become straight, the rough ways smooth. And all people will see God's salvation."

Luke 3:5–6

The LORD will indeed give what is good, and our land will yield its harvest. Righteousness goes before him and prepares the way for his steps.

Psalm 85:12–13

Thoughts for Today

Thank God for the battle verses in the Bible. We go into the unknown every day of our lives, and especially every Monday morning, for the week is sure to be a battlefield, outwardly and inwardly in the unseen life of the spirit, which is often by far the sternest battlefield for souls. Either way, the Lord your God goes before you. He shall fight for you!

Amy Carmichael

One on God's side is a majority.

Wendell Phillips

How often we look upon God as our last and feeblest resource! We go to Him because we have nowhere else to go. And then we learn that the storms of life have driven us, not upon the rocks, but into the desired haven.

George MacDonald

A Prayer for Today

Father in Heaven, You see the challenges in my life and where the odds are stacked high against me. There are giants in front of me, but I'm not worried about them. I acknowledge that the battle will not be won by my own strength or by my own power. I will accomplish this because You hold my future in Your hands. You will go before me, fighting my battles and making the crooked places straight. I believe that You have the final say, and You have promised You will cross over ahead of me and defeat my challenges for me.

Takeaway Truth

God will not stop every adversity.

He will not prevent every challenge. But

if we will stay in faith, He promises He

will bring us through every challenge and

get us wherever we're supposed to be.

Almighty God holds your future in His

hands, goes before you, fights your bat-

tles, and makes crooked places straight.

CHAPTER
10

The Gracious Hand of God

> **Key Truth**
>
> God put something in you to give you an advantage—His favor, His blessing, "the gracious hand of God."

When God breathed His life into you, He put something in you to give you an advantage. There is something about you that makes you stand out, something that draws opportunity, something that causes you to overcome obstacles, to accomplish dreams. The Scripture calls it "the gracious hand of God." You can't put your finger on it. But you know this is not just your talent, your education, or your hard work. It's Almighty God breathing in your direction. You could call it "the favor factor."

Like me, you may wonder sometimes, "How did I get to where I am? This was not just my own ability." My mother often asks, "How did I overcome that sickness when the medical report said no way?" You may think, "How could I be this happy, this blessed, after all I've been through?" That's not just good fortune, not just a lucky break. That's the gracious hand of God giving you His favor and His blessing on your life.

Perhaps Nehemiah demonstrates this principle the best in the Scripture. When he heard that the walls of Jerusalem had been torn down, God put a dream in his heart to rebuild those walls. In the natural it was impossible. He was living more than a thousand miles away, working as a cupbearer to the king. He didn't have the money, the manpower, or the influence. On paper he didn't have a chance. But Nehemiah knew he had the favor factor.

When he asked the king for permission to take a leave of absence to go back to Jerusalem and build those walls, the king not only said yes but he gave Nehemiah letters of protection and the materials he needed to complete the task. Nehemiah 2:8 tells us why this happened. Nehemiah said "the gracious hand of my God was on me." Even though he had no experience or the resources and faced untold opposition in rebuilding the walls, the favor of God helped him to overcome them. It should have taken them at least a year to complete the walls, but they did it in just fifty-two days.

When you realize God's hand of favor is upon you, you will accomplish your dreams faster than you ever thought possible. You may be facing a situation like Nehemiah that seems impossible. Don't go around talking about how big the problem is, or how you're never going to make it. God's gracious hand is on you. You have the favor factor, so don't keep dwelling on everything you lack, the mistakes you've made, or the greater talents of the competition. You're just looking in the natural, at what's on paper, but there is something about you that cannot be measured, something that goes beyond your talent, your education, or your ability.

It's the favor of Almighty God.

Quit telling yourself the wall is too big, the dream is too great, or the obstacles are too high. It will not happen in your own strength. It will not happen in your own power. It will happen because Almighty God favors you.

Consider This

To live with the gracious hand of God upon you—can you describe what that looks like? How might God bring opportunities across your path that are greater than you can imagine?

....
....
....
....
....
....
....
....
....
....
....
....
....
....
....
....
....
....
....
....

What the Scriptures Say

"The gracious hand of our God is on everyone who looks to him . . ."

Ezra 8:22

When his master saw that the LORD was with him and that the LORD gave him success in everything he did, Joseph found favor in his eyes and became his attendant. Potiphar put him in charge of his household, and he entrusted to his care everything he owned.

Genesis 39:3–4

Thoughts for Today

Try claiming God's blessings instead
of merely longing for them.

Henry Jacobsen

Every calling is great when greatly pursued.

Oliver Wendell Holmes Jr.

So [God] supplies perfectly measured grace to meet
the needs of the godly. For daily needs there is daily grace;
for sudden needs, sudden grace; for overwhelming need, overwhelming grace. God's grace is given wonderfully, but not
wastefully; freely but not foolishly; bountifully but not blindly.

John Blanchard

....

....

....

....

....

....

....

....

....

....

....

....

....

A Prayer for Today

Father, thank You that Your gracious hand is upon me.
I know I have an advantage. I have an edge. Other people
may not see it. They may try to push me down and dis-
qualify me. But that's okay. I know the truth. I have the
favor factor. I'm well able to fulfill my destiny.

Takeaway Truth

You have this favor factor. There is something about you that can't be put on paper. The bottom line is, you've got what it takes. Now do your part and activate this favor. When the dream looks too big, don't give up. Be like Nehemiah and say, "Lord, thank You that Your gracious hand is upon me." You will become everything God has created you to be, and you will have everything God intended for you to have.

Part III:
Pray God-Sized Prayers

CHAPTER
11

Pray God-Sized Prayers

> ### *Key Truth*
> When you have the boldness to ask God for big things, you will see the greatness of God's power.

How you pray determines what kind of life you live. If you only pray small, ordinary, get-by prayers, then you'll live a small, ordinary, get-by life. But when you have the boldness to ask God for big things, you ask Him to open doors that might otherwise never open. You ask Him to take you further than anyone in your family. You ask Him to restore a relationship that looks over and done.

When you pray God-sized prayers, you will see the greatness of God's power. All through the Scripture we see this principle. Elijah prayed that it wouldn't rain, and for three and a half years there was no rain. Joshua prayed for more daylight, and God stopped the sun. Elisha prayed for protection, and his enemies standing right in front of him didn't recognize him. God made him invisible.

The common denominator is that they asked God to do the unthinkable. If you're to reach your highest potential, you have to have this same boldness. When was the last time you asked God to do something impossible or something out of the ordinary? One reason we don't see God do great things is that we ask only for small things.

Most people pray over their food. They pray for protection. They ask God for wisdom. That's all good, but it's limiting what God can do. There should be something you're praying about and asking for that seems impossible, far out, something that you cannot achieve on your own.

The phrase I hear in my spirit is *Dare to ask*. Your dream may seem impossible. You may feel you don't have the connections or the funding, but God is saying, "Dare to ask Me to bring it to pass. Dare to ask Me to connect you to the right people. Dare to ask Me to pour out a flood of My favor."

I wonder how many of your prayers are not being answered simply because you're not asking. You may tell yourself: "God is God. If He wants to bless me, He'll bless me." But the Scripture says in James 4:2, "You do not have because you do not ask God." If you're not asking big, then you're shortchanging yourself. You will never reach your highest potential if you pray only small prayers.

I believe one reason I've seen God's favor in my life is that I've learned to ask big. When my father died and I had never ministered before, I prayed a bold prayer asking God to help me not only to maintain what my parents have built, but also for God to let me go further. It was a bold prayer when I walked in that jewelry store, met Victoria for the first time, and prayed: "God, please let her see how good-looking I am!" It was a bold prayer to ask God to help us build our church in the arena where the Rockets used to play basketball.

It's good to ask God for your needs, but I'm challenging you to ask for your dreams. Quit asking small. Quit acting like you're bothering God. Quit praying weak, get-by prayers. Your Father owns it all. He created the universe. If you want to see the fullness of what He has in store, you should learn to ask big.

Consider This

—◇—

The Scripture says, "It is your Father's good pleasure
to give you the kingdom" (Luke 12:32 NKJV). God wants to
give you the desires of your heart, but you have to have
the faith of a child and be willing to ask. What God-sized
prayer are you asking Him for today?

....

....

....

....

....

....

....

....

....

....

....

....

....

....

....

....

....

....

....

What the Scriptures Say

"And now, LORD, let the promise you have made
concerning your servant and his house be established forever.
Do as you promised, so that it will be established and that your
name will be great forever. . . . You, my God, have revealed
to your servant that you will build a house for him. So your
servant has found courage to pray to you. You, LORD, are God!
You have promised these good things to your servant. Now you
have been pleased to bless the house of your servant, that
it may continue forever in your sight; for you, LORD,
have blessed it, and it will be blessed forever."

1 Chronicles 17:23–27

"Ask me, and I will make the nations your inheritance,
the ends of the earth your possession."

Psalm 2:8

Thoughts for Today

Pray for great things, expect great things,
work for great things, but above all, pray.

R. A. Torrey

Prayer is not overcoming God's reluctance:
it is laying hold of His highest willingness.

Richard Chenevix Trench

Prayer moves the hand that moves the world.

John A. Wallace

A Prayer for Today

Father, You have promised to give us the desires of our hearts. I have dreams in my heart that seem impossible. But You promised it, and now I'm bold enough to ask You for it. I can't do this on my own, but I know You are all-powerful. You have no limitations. There is nothing too difficult for You, so God, I'm asking for Your favor to shine down on me. I'm asking You to make a way, even though I don't see a way. God, I'm asking You to open doors that no man can shut.

Takeaway Truth

When you face situations that seem impossible in your everyday life, God says, "I dare you to pray." When you ask, God releases favor. When you ask, angels go to work. When you ask, strongholds are broken. When you ask, the Most High God begins to breathe in your direction. When you pray God-sized prayers, you will see the greatness of God's power.

CHAPTER
12

Remind God of What He Said

> ### *Key Truth*
> One of the most powerful ways
> to pray is to find a promise in the
> Scripture and remind God what
> He said about you.

M y sister Lisa and her husband, Kevin, had been trying to have a baby for six years with no success. Isaiah 41 says, "Present your case before God. Make your arguments. Bring forth your proof," so she listed on a piece of paper all of the promises she was standing on concerning having a baby. She made it like a legal contract with God.

"God, Kevin and I are presenting our case to You based on Your Word. You said in Genesis 1:28 to be fruitful and multiply. You said in Psalm 112 our children would be mighty in the land. You said in Psalm 113 that You make the barren woman a happy mother of children. God, we've done all we know how to do. Now we're presenting our case based on Your Word, knowing that You are faithful and true to what You have said."

She took the contract and placed it on her bathroom mirror where she could see it. Again and again, week after week, month after month, she just kept reminding God what He had promised. About two years later, God blessed them with twins, and today they have three beautiful children. God is faithful to His Word.

One of the most powerful ways to pray is to find a promise in the Scripture and remind God what He said about you. Isaiah 62:6–7 says in effect, "Put God in remembrance of His promises. Keep not silent. Give Him no rest till it comes to pass." When God hears His promises, He dispatches angels with the answers. He sets the miracle into motion. He will change things in your favor. It may not happen overnight, but just stay in faith and keep reminding God what He promised you day in and day out.

Notice that it doesn't say, "Put God in remembrance of your *problems.*" Sometimes we use prayer as an excuse to complain: "God, these people at work are not treating me right." Or, "God, these gas prices are so high I don't know how I'm going to make it." Or, "God, these children are getting on my nerves. I can't take it anymore."

Instead of complaining, remind Him: "God, You said . . ." Instead of begging, remind Him: "God, You said . . ." Instead of describing the circumstances, bring up His promises: "God, You said . . ." Don't keep silent. Remind God again and again. Then eventually you will see what God said come to pass in your life.

My questions are: Are you presenting your case? Do you have any proof? Have you done as Lisa did and found the promise He made so you can say, "God, You said . . ."?

If you present your case before God, the good news is that Jesus is called our "Advocate." Another word for advocate is "lawyer." In the courtroom of Heaven, imagine Jesus is our lawyer. God is the judge. Don't tell God why you can't be successful, why you can't get well, why you'll never get out of debt. Present your case based on God's Word and you cannot lose. He will be faithful and true to His Word.

Consider This

In Luke 18:1–8, Jesus told a parable about an unfair, unjust judge who finally was willing to listen to a woman's case because of her "continual coming" or "shameless persistence." That's the way we need to be when it comes to reminding God of what He said. What promise or promises from God are you bringing to His constant remembrance?

What the Scriptures Say

Remember your word to your servant,
for you have given me hope.

Psalm 119:49

"Now, Lord, the God of Israel, keep for your servant
David my father the promises you made to him when you said,
'You shall never fail to have a successor to sit before me on the
throne of Israel, if only your descendants are careful in all they
do to walk before me according to my law, as you have done.'
And now, Lord, the God of Israel, let your word that you
promised your servant David come true."

2 Chronicles 6:16–17

Thoughts for Today

—◇—

Asking with shameless persistence, the importunity that
will not be denied, returns with the answer in hand.

Author Unknown

It is the nature of faith to believe God upon His bare word. . . .
It will not be, says sense; it cannot be, says reason; it both
can and will be, says faith, for I have a promise for it.

John Trapp

There is no saint here who can out-believe God.
God never out-promised Himself yet.

C. H. Spurgeon

A Prayer for Today

Father God, You said You would supply all of my needs according to Your riches. You are Jehovah Jireh, the Lord my provider. You said what is impossible with men is possible with You. You said my end would be better than my beginning. You said all things are going to work together for my good. Thank You that You are faithful to Your Word and will work mightily in my behalf.

Takeaway Truth

If you put God in remembrance of His promises

and do not put Him in remembrance of your

problems, then He will be faithful to His Word.

Go to Him in faith with a *You said.*

What God promised, He will do.

CHAPTER
13

Power of Believing

> ### *Key Truth*
> When you get in agreement
> with God and believe what He says
> about you, then what you believe
> can supersede any natural law.

One of the greatest abilities God has given each of us is our ability to believe. If you believe, you can be successful. If you believe, you can overcome mistakes of the past. If you believe, you can fulfill your God-given destiny. There is incredible power in what we believe.

What you believe is greater than what the medical report says. We respect medical science, but God has the final say. When you get in agreement with God and believe what He says about you, then what you believe can supersede any natural law.

What you believe is greater than what is in your bank account. I have a friend who came to this country with nothing but the clothes on his back. Today, he runs a Fortune 500 company. Against all odds, he believed he could do what God put in his heart.

Paul prayed in Ephesians 1:19 that we would understand the incredible greatness of God's power for those who believe. Notice the power is activated only when we believe. That means right now the Creator of the universe is just waiting to release healing, restoration, favor, promotion, and abundance. The only catch is that we have to believe.

It's not complicated. God didn't say, "If you will pray three hours a day," or, "If you'll quote twelve chapters in the Scripture, then I'll do it for you." No, He said, "If you will only believe." In other words, if you will just get your mind going in the right direction and believe you can rise higher. Believe you can overcome the obstacle. Believe your family can be restored. Believe you can do something great and make your mark in this generation.

When you believe, the surpassing greatness of God's power is released. You may have to develop new habits. If you've been negative for a long time, you should retrain your thinking from "I can't" to "I can." From "It won't happen" to "It will happen." From "I'll never get well" to "God is restoring health unto me."

Reprogram your computer. Load in some new software. First Chronicles 28:20 says don't be discouraged by the size of the task, for the Lord your God is with you. He will see to it that it is finished completely.

When you believe, God will see to it that it's taken care of. When you believe, you have the Creator of the universe fighting your battles, arranging things in your favor, going before you, moving the wrong people out of the way. You couldn't have made it happen in your own strength, but because you are a believer, the surpassing greatness of God's power is at work in your life.

Let this take root in your spirit. Because you are a believer, all will be well with you. All will be well with your family. All will be well with your finances. All will be well in your health. All will be well with your career. You need to get ready, because God's promises are about to come to pass in your life.

It may not happen on your timetable. When Lazarus was sick, Jesus did not come until after he had died. That's because God was planning a resurrection rather than a healing. Keep believing. It will be better, bigger, and greater than you've ever imagined.

Consider This

———◇———

Isaiah 3:10 says, "Tell the righteous it will be well with them." You may go through some difficulties. You may have been praying, believing for your situation to change for a long time, but you don't see anything happening. God is working behind the scenes right now arranging things in your favor. The answer is already on the way. What is it that you need to keep believing God for?

....
....
....
....
....
....
....
....
....
....
....
....
....
....
....
....
....

What the Scriptures Say

"Lord," Martha said to Jesus, "if you had been here, my brother would not have died. But I know that even now God will give you whatever you ask." Jesus said to her, "Your brother will rise again." Martha answered, "I know he will rise again in the resurrection at the last day." Jesus said to her, "I am the resurrection and the life. The one who believes in me will live, even though they die; and whoever lives by believing in me will never die. Do you believe this?"

John 11:21–26

While Jesus was still speaking, some people came from the house of Jairus, the synagogue leader. "Your daughter is dead," they said. "Why bother the teacher anymore?" Overhearing what they said, Jesus told him, "Don't be afraid; just believe."

Mark 5:35–36

Thoughts for Today

— ◇ —

Faith is the subtle chain that binds us to the infinite.

O. E. Smith

Faith is not shelter against difficulties,
but belief in the face of all contradictions.

Paul Tournier

The steps of faith fall on the seeming
void and find the rock beneath.

Walt Whitman

....
....
....
....
....
....
....
....
....
....
....
....
....
....

A Prayer for Today

Father God, when You put a promise in my heart that seems impossible, I want to learn to respond with three simple words, "Lord, I believe." I want to get into agreement with You and see the incredible greatness of Your power activated. You are my Jehovah Jireh, the Lord my provider. You are still on the Throne. I believe that with one touch of Your favor I'll go from barely making it to having more than enough.

Takeaway Truth

Be a believer. Take the limits off God. There is so much more to our God. Don't keep Him in a little box. Discover what else He is. Keep your faith stirred up. I believe and declare you are going to see God's goodness in amazing ways!

CHAPTER
14

Have Uncommon Faith

> ### *Key Truth*
> Uncommon faith believes above and beyond and gives you a boldness and a confidence to believe for the extraordinary.

My father was raised in extreme poverty. His parents lost everything they had during the Great Depression. My father had no money, no education at the time, no future to speak of. But at the age of seventeen, he gave his life to Christ. God put a dream in his heart that one day he would minister to people around the world. In the natural it looked totally impossible. He had no connections, no way to get out of that limited environment. All he had was this uncommon faith. He dared to ask God for the right breaks and the right opportunities.

Years later, as we traveled together in India, in the jungles of Thailand, and in villages along the Amazon River, I watched people recognize my father and hold up their Bibles and tell in their own language what they'd heard him write in his books and say on his tapes, videos, and television broadcasts. How could it be that my father could fulfill his dream and not only touch people here but people all over the world?

My father had this uncommon faith. He did not settle where many others would have settled. When all the odds were against him, instead of giving up, he believed that God would make a way. He was bold enough to ask for God's favor. He saw God take him places that he never even dreamed of.

Uncommon faith is not average faith. It's not ordinary. It's above and beyond. It gives you a boldness and a confidence to believe for the extraordinary. It is radical faith. It's extreme. You believe God can do anything. You don't make little plans.

Average faith says, "God, help me to survive this recession." Uncommon faith says, "God, I believe You will prosper me right in the midst of this recession." Average faith says, "Maybe one day I'll get out of this problem. I don't know. It's pretty bad." Uncommon faith says, "I know I'm not only coming out, I'm coming out better off than I was before."

I want to light a new fire under you. There is no obstacle too difficult for you to overcome. No dreams put in your heart by God are too big to accomplish. Ask yourself, "Is my faith radical? Is what I'm believing for, the vision for my life, is it big enough to make someone think, 'What's his problem? Who does he think he is?'" Or, are you stuck in a rut and just accepting where you are as the way it will always be?

One time Joshua was in the midst of a great battle. He and his men were trying to finish off this army, but the sun was going down. Joshua knew that if he couldn't get this army totally defeated, then later on they would rise up and cause him problems. So he asked God to stop the sun, something that had never been done before, and God did. When you have this uncommon faith, it brings a smile to God's face. God interrupted the entire universe just because one man had uncommon faith.

Have you ever asked God for something out of the ordinary? Don't you think it's time to do so?

Consider This

If you study the Prophet Elisha's life, you'll find that
he asked for a double portion of Elijah's spirit when
Elijah was going to Heaven, and that was exactly
what happened. He did twice the miracles. He had
a double portion of his anointing. He dared to ask.
In what ways are you taking the limits off God and
releasing your faith in uncommon ways?

What the Scriptures Say

On the day the LORD gave the Amorites over to Israel, Joshua said to the LORD in the presence of Israel: "Sun, stand still over Gibeon, and you, moon, over the Valley of Aijalon.". . . The sun stopped in the middle of the sky and delayed going down about a full day. There has never been a day like it before or since, a day when the LORD listened to a human being.

Joshua 10:12–14

Shortly before dawn Jesus went out to them, walking on the lake. When the disciples saw him walking on the lake, they were terrified. . . . But Jesus immediately said to them: "Take courage! It is I. Don't be afraid." "Lord, if it's you," Peter replied, "tell me to come to you on the water." "Come," he said. Then Peter got down out of the boat, walked on the water and came toward Jesus.

Matthew 14:25–29

Thoughts for Today

God loves with a great love the man whose heart is
bursting with a passion for the impossible.

William Booth

True faith rests upon the character of God and asks
no further proof than the moral perfections of the
One who cannot lie. It is enough that God has said it.

A. W. Tozer

Faith is a living, daring confidence in God's grace,
so sure and certain that a man could stake
his life on it a thousand times.

Martin Luther

....

....

....

....

....

....

....

....

....

....

....

....

....

A Prayer for Today

Father, I would like to join Joshua and Elisha and Peter and put a smile on Your face by taking the limits off of You and releasing my faith in uncommon ways. I want to step out of the boat and believe You for the extraordinary. I want to believe that You will increase me and show me Your favor. I believe that You are taking me forward into the fullness of my destiny.

Takeaway Truth

If you are not stretching your faith, you're

not tapping into everything God has in store.

Take the limits off God and release your faith

in uncommon ways, and you will see

God do uncommon things.

Part IV:
Keep the Right Perspective

CHAPTER
15

Keep the Right Perspective

> ### *Key Truth*
> We all face challenges, but it's not the size of the problem that's important, it's our perception of that problem; it's how big or small we make it in our minds.

When Moses sent twelve men to spy out the Promised Land, ten came back and said, "We'll never defeat them. There are giants in the land." But the two other spies, Joshua and Caleb, came back with a different report. They said, "Yes, the people are big, but our God is bigger. We are well able to take the land. Let us go in at once."

Both groups saw the same giants and the same situation; the only difference was their perspective. One group focused on the size of their God, the other group focused on the size of their enemy. Out of the two million people camped next door to the Promised Land, only two made it in, Joshua and Caleb. Could it be that your perspective is keeping you out of your promised land? If you see your challenges as impossible and you tell yourself, "I'll never get out of debt, and I'll never overcome this sickness, and I'll never accomplish my dreams," then just like them, your wrong perspective can keep you from becoming all God's created you to be.

What you focus on, you magnify. If you stay focused on your problem or what you don't have and how it will never work out, all you're doing is making it bigger than it really is. When you magnify something, you don't change the size of the object; you only change your perception of it.

That was why David said, "Magnify the Lord with me." He was saying if you want to make something bigger, then don't make your problems bigger, don't make the medical report bigger, don't make the opposition bigger. Learn instead to make God bigger.

When David faced Goliath, he never called him a giant. Everybody else did. They talked about his size, his strength, and his skill. But David called Goliath an uncircumcised Philistine. He never even gave him credit for being that big. Here's the key: David didn't deny it, but he didn't dwell on it. His attitude was: "I'm not focusing on how big my problems are. I'm focusing on how big my God is." This teenage boy—half the giant's size with no chance in the natural—defeated this huge giant. How? He had the right perspective.

Philippians 1:28 (NLT) says, "Don't be intimidated in any way by your enemies." You may be like David, up against a big giant right now; a giant of debt, a giant of sickness, a giant legal problem. It looks impossible in the natural. But God is saying, "Don't be intimidated. Those for you are greater than those against you. Put your shoulders back and hold your head up high. You are not weak, defeated, or powerless; you are a child of the Most High God, anointed, equipped, well able. Don't you dare shrink back and think, 'It's just too big.'"

Do as David did—get a new perspective. You are full of can-do power. The greatest force in the universe is breathing in your direction. The same power that raised Christ from the dead lives on inside of you. There is no challenge too tough for you, no enemy too big, no sickness too great, and no dream too far off.

Consider This

——◇——

Do you know what made David king? Goliath. God
used the opposition to take him to the throne. When
you face great difficulties, it's because God wants to
take you to your throne. He wants to take you to a
higher level. What challenge are you facing that God
wants to use to your advantage?

....

....

....

....

....

....

....

....

....

....

....

....

....

....

....

....

....

....

What the Scriptures Say

"Behold, I give unto you power to tread on serpents and scorpions, and over all the power of the enemy: and nothing shall by any means hurt you."

Luke 10:19 KJV

When the servant of the man of God got up and went out early the next morning, an army with horses and chariots had surrounded the city. "Oh no, my lord! What shall we do?" the servant asked. "Don't be afraid," the prophet answered. "Those who are with us are more than those who are with them." And Elisha prayed, "Open his eyes, LORD, so that he may see." Then the LORD opened the servant's eyes, and he looked and saw the hills full of horses and chariots of fire all around Elisha.

2 Kings 6:15–17

Thoughts for Today

All our difficulties are only platforms for the manifestations of God's grace, power, and love.

Hudson Taylor

If anyone would tell you the shortest, surest way to happiness, he must tell you to make it a rule to yourself to thank and praise God for everything that happens to you. For it is certain that whatever seeming calamity happens to you, if you thank and praise God for it, you turn it into a blessing.

William Law

Adversity causes some men to break;
others to break records.

William A. Ward

A Prayer for Today

Father, thank You that I am a child of the Most High God,
anointed, equipped, and well able to overcome. I am not weak,
defeated, or powerless. I will not be intimidated, shrink back
and think my problems are too big. The same power that raised
Christ from the dead lives on inside of me. You are greater
than anything that is against me, and You control my destiny.
No weapon formed against me will prosper. I believe that it's
just a matter of time before I break through to a new level.

Takeaway Truth

If you are facing a big giant challenge, don't focus on the size of the problem; focus on the size of your God. He's brought you through in the past, and He will bring you through in the future. God has something amazing just up in front of you. He has a new level of your destiny. God will not only bring you out, He will bring you out better off than you were before!

CHAPTER
16

Stay in the Game

> ### *Key Truth*
> If you are to become all God created you to be, you can't let a hurt, a loss, a bad break, or disappointment cause you to sit on the sidelines.

It's easy to have a good attitude and pursue your dreams as long as everything is going your way. But what about the difficult times when a relationship doesn't work out, you get a bad health report, or a friend does you wrong? It's easy to lose your passion when you are hurting. Many people are sitting on the sidelines of life, nursing their wounds and not moving forward because of what they've been through.

You may have a *reason* to feel sorry for yourself, but you don't have a *right*. God promised to give you beauty for those ashes. He said He would pay you back double for the wrongs, but you have to do your part. If you are to see the beauty, if you're to get double, you have to shake off the discouragement and get back in the game. We all have wounds, but you can't let a loss, a health issue, or a divorce be your excuse to sit on the sidelines. Sometimes in life you have to play in pain.

God rewards faithful people. People who are determined. People who get knocked down, but don't stay down. Instead, they get back up again. You can't let the hurt, the pain, or the bad break cause you to be bitter, or to lose your passion, or to start blaming God.

One of the best things you can do when you're hurting is go out and help somebody else who is hurting. Get your mind off your problems and pain by helping somebody else in need. When you help others in your time of need, you are sowing a seed God can use to change your situation.

This was what my mother did in 1981, when she was diagnosed with terminal liver cancer and given a few weeks to live. She didn't feel well. She had a good reason to be discouraged. She could have gone home, pulled the curtains, and been depressed. She could have sat on the sidelines. Nobody would have faulted her. But my mother understood this principle. She stayed in the game. She would drive across town to pray for a sick friend. The truth is she needed prayer more than that friend, but my mother was sowing a seed. She would come to church every weekend and pray for other people in need. She was hurting, but she was still in the game.

Isaiah put it this way, "Arise from the depression in which the circumstances have kept you. Rise to a new life." Notice, if you want a new life, there's something you have to do. You can't sit back in self-pity. Shake off what didn't work out. Quit mourning over what you've lost. Quit dwelling on who hurt you and how unfair it was, and rise to a new life. There is still life after the sickness, life after the divorce, and life after the bad break. A full life is still in front of you. You have not danced your best dance. You have not laughed your best laugh. You have not dreamed your best dream.

If you stay in the game and do not grow bitter, God will always have an "after this" for you. He will bring you out and pay you back for the wrongs that have happened to you.

Consider This

The Scripture says Job went through unthinkably tough times. Everything that could go wrong did—the loss of his wealth, his children, and his health. But in the midst of that pain, Job said, "I know my Redeemer lives." Job remained faithful to God, and when he came through that challenge, God paid him back double for what he lost. Maybe you've suffered a loss, been through a disappointment. How can you arise and get back in the game?

What the Scriptures Say

He has sent me to bind up the brokenhearted, to proclaim
freedom for the captives and release from darkness for the
prisoners, to proclaim the year of the LORD's favor . . . , to
comfort all who mourn, and provide for those who grieve
in Zion—to bestow on them a crown of beauty instead of
ashes, the oil of joy instead of mourning, and a garment
of praise instead of a spirit of despair.

Isaiah 61:1–3

At this [hearing about the loss of his children], Job got
up and tore his robe and shaved his head. Then he fell to the
ground in worship and said: ". . . The LORD gave and the LORD
has taken away; may the name of the LORD be praised."

Job 1:20–21

Thoughts for Today

While women weep, as they do now, I'll fight; while little children go hungry, I'll fight; while men go to prison, in and out, in and out, as they do now, I'll fight; while there is a drunkard left, while there is a poor lost girl upon the streets, where there remains one dark soul without the light of God—I'll fight! I'll fight to the very end!

William Booth

What then are we to do about our problems? We must learn to live with them until such time as God delivers us from them. We must pray for grace to endure them without murmuring. Problems patiently endured will work for our spiritual perfecting. They harm us only when we resist them or endure them unwillingly.

A. W. Tozer

God will not permit any troubles to come upon us, unless He has a specific plan by which great blessing can come out of the difficulty.

Peter Marshall

. . . .
. . . .
. . . .
. . . .
. . . .
. . . .
. . . .

A Prayer for Today

Father, You have promised to take the scars of my life and turn them into stars, to give me beauty for ashes, and to pay me back double for anything lost. I have made up my mind to stay in the game, knowing You restore health and give new opportunities and new relationships and new perspectives. Even though it's painful for a time, it is not the end. A full life is still in front of me. I believe You have an "after this" in my future.

Takeaway Truth

You may be in pain today. Maybe you've suffered a

loss, been through a disappointment. That is not the

end. God still has a plan. Don't sit around nursing your

wounds. Don't let bitterness and discouragement set

the tone for your life. God is saying, "Arise. Wipe away

the tears and get back in the game." God is going to

make the rest of your life the best of your life.

CHAPTER
17

Your Second Wind Is on Its Way

> ### *Key Truth*
> When you become weary and feel like quitting, there is a way to have your strength renewed—wait on the Lord.

We all grow tired sometimes, tired of trying to make a business grow, tired of dealing with a sickness, tired of raising a difficult child, tired of being lonely and waiting to meet the right person. We can even be doing what we love, but if we're not careful, we can lose our passion and allow weariness to set in.

On the way to our victories we will always face the weariness test. We will be tempted to become discouraged and give up. The test never comes when we're fresh. It never comes when we first start out. It always comes when we're tired. That's when we're the most vulnerable.

The Apostle Paul said, "Let us not be weary in well doing: for in due season we shall reap, if we faint not" (Galatians 6:9 KJV). Two words are the key to this whole passage; "faint not." In other words, if you don't give up, if you shake off the weariness, if you put on a new attitude knowing that God is still in control, if you dig your heels in and say, "I've come too far to stop now," if you "faint not," you will see the promise come to pass.

We all become weary. In fact, if you never feel like giving up, then your dreams are too small. If you never feel like quitting, then you need to set some larger goals. When that pressure comes to be discouraged and to think you can't take it anymore, that is completely normal. Every person feels that way at times.

Isaiah gives us the solution. He said, "Those who wait on the LORD shall renew their strength; they shall mount up with wings like eagles, they will run and not be weary, they shall walk and not faint" (Isaiah 40:31 NKJV). God knew there would be times when we would feel battle fatigue. That's why He said, "There is a way to get your second wind. There is a way to have your strength renewed. What is it? Wait on the Lord."

One translation says, "Hope in the Lord." That doesn't mean to sit around and be passive, complacent. It means to wait with expectancy, not complaining, not discouraged, not talking about all the reasons why it won't work out.

If you want your strength renewed, the right way to wait is to give God praise, to talk about His greatness; you go through the day expecting Him to turn it around. God promises He will renew your strength. The Scripture says, "You will run and not get weary." This is a reference to catching your second wind. That's God breathing strength, energy, passion, vision, and vitality back into your spirit. You won't just come out the way you were. You will come out on wings like eagles. You will come out stronger, higher, better off than you were before.

Your challenge may be difficult, but you can handle it. God has given you the grace for this season. If you weren't up to this, God wouldn't have brought it across your path. In tough times remind yourself there is always a reward for doing right. God never fails to compensate you. He pays very well. The season may be difficult right now, but if you keep doing the right thing, get ready because the reward is coming.

Consider This

The word *weary* means "to lose the sense of pleasure, to not feel the enjoyment that you once felt." Perhaps the battle you are facing has lasted longer than you thought it would. You've prayed. You've believed. You've done what you're supposed to, but there it is. How will you shake off the weariness and see God's promises come to pass?

What the Scriptures Say

Though the fig tree does not bud and there are no
grapes on the vines, though the olive crop fails and
the fields produce no food, . . . yet I will rejoice in the
LORD, I will be joyful in God my Savior. The Sovereign
LORD is my strength; he makes my feet like the feet of a
deer, he enables me to tread on the heights.

Habakkuk 3:17–19

"Come to me, all you who are weary and burdened,
and I will give you rest. Take my yoke upon you and
learn from me, for I am gentle and humble in heart,
and you will find rest for your souls."

Matthew 11:28–29

Thoughts for Today

There are two ways of getting out of a trial.
One is simply to try to get rid of the trial, and be thankful
when it is over. The other is to recognize the trial as a
challenge from God to claim a larger blessing than we have
ever had, and to hail it with delight as an opportunity of
obtaining a larger measure of divine grace.

A. B. Simpson

Do not let your happiness depend on something you may
lose . . . only (upon) the Beloved who will never pass away.

C. S. Lewis

Life is a hard fight, a struggle, a wrestling with the principle
of evil . . . Every inch of the way must be disputed. The
night is given us to take breath, to pray, to drink deep at
the fountain of power. The day, to use the strength that has
been given us, to go forth to work with it till the evening.

Florence Nightingale

A Prayer for Today

Father God, You said You have armed me with strength for every battle. You said I can do all things through Christ who infuses inner strength into me. You said I am more than a conqueror, a victor and not a victim. Thank You that You are fighting my battles. Thank You that the answer is on the way. Thank You that You are bigger than these obstacles. Thank You that You are bringing my dreams to pass.

Takeaway Truth

I believe right now the Creator of the
universe is breathing a second wind into you.
Just receive it by faith. Strength is coming
into your body. Strength is coming into your
mind. You will run and not grow weary. You
will walk and not faint. You will not drag
through life defeated or depressed. You will
soar through life on wings like eagles!

CHAPTER
18

The God Who Closes Doors

> ### Key Truth
> A big part of faith is trusting God when you don't understand why things happen the way they do.

We all know that God opens doors. We've seen Him give us favor, good breaks, promotion. That's the hand of God opening the door. But the same God who opens doors will close doors.

Maybe you prayed, but you didn't get a promotion you wanted. You applied, but your loan application didn't go through. A relationship you'd enjoyed didn't work out. So often we can become discouraged and feel like God has let us down.

But God can see the big picture for your life. God knows where every road is leading. He knows the dead ends. He can see the shortcuts. He knows some roads are a big circle.

We would go for years and end up right back where we started, never making any progress. We can't see what God can see. A big part of faith is trusting God when you don't understand why things happen the way they do. God may close a door because you're believing too small. If He opened the door, it would limit what He wants to do in your life. Another door may close because it's not the right time, or there are other people involved and they're not ready yet. If God opened that door at the wrong time, it wouldn't work out.

The bottom line is: God has your best interests at heart. When a door closes, you don't know what God is saving you from. If your prayers aren't answered the way you want, instead of being discouraged or feeling like God let you down, why don't you have a bigger perspective? The reason the door closed is because God has something better in store.

First Corinthians 13:12 (NKJV) says, "For now we see in a mirror, dimly, but then face to face." Right now you may not see all clearly. You're only looking at it in part. But one day it will come into focus, and you'll look back and say, "Wow, God! You are amazing! You had it all figured out. You closed the door on purpose so Your perfect will would be done."

That's what happened to this one bright young man who was in the top five percent of the nation. His dream was to become an engineer. However, when he applied to do graduate studies at about a dozen or so of the best engineering schools in the nation, he was turned down again and again while some of his friends with lower grades and scores were accepted. He could not understand it.

While he was waiting, he went on a mission trip with a group of doctors from his church. When he saw the doctors taking care of the people, treating their diseases, something new was birthed on the inside. He thought, "I don't want to be an engineer. This is what I want to do with my life." After he returned home, he applied to medical school and was immediately accepted. God closed the doors to the engineering school on purpose, to push him into his divine destiny.

You may be discouraged because your plans have not worked out, but those closed doors were not an accident. That was God directing your steps. The reason God closed them is because He has something better in store. Will you trust Him?

Consider This

The Scripture says, "God's ways are not our ways. They are better than our ways." There will be times when a door closes and you can't understand why. You may be experiencing that right now. Here's the question: Will you stay in faith while you wait to see what God is up to?

What the Scriptures Say

"For my thoughts are not your thoughts, neither are your ways my ways," declares the LORD. "As the heavens are higher than the earth, so are my ways higher than your ways and my thoughts than your thoughts."

Isaiah 55:8–9

"These are the words of him who is holy and true, who holds the key of David. What he opens no one can shut, and what he shuts no one can open. I know your deeds. See, I have placed before you an open door that no one can shut."

Revelation 3:7–8

....

....

....

....

....

....

....

....

....

....

....

....

....

....

Thoughts for Today

God is wonderful in His design and excellent in
His working. Believer, God overrules all things for your good.
The needs-be for all that you have suffered has been most
accurately determined by God. Your course is all mapped out
by your Lord. Nothing will take Him by surprise. There will be
no novelties to Him. There will be no occurrences which He
did not foresee, and for which, therefore, He has not provided.
He has arranged all, and you have but to patiently wait,
and you shall sing a song of deliverance.

C. H. Spurgeon

Real satisfaction comes not in understanding God's motives,
but in understanding His character, in trusting in His promises,
and in leaning on Him and resting in Him as the Sovereign
who knows what He is doing and does all things well.

Joni Eareckson Tada

When a train goes through a tunnel and it gets dark,
you don't throw away the ticket and jump off.
You sit still and trust the engineer.

Corrie ten Boom

. . . .
. . . .
. . . .
. . . .
. . . .
. . . .

A Prayer for Today

Father God, You are amazing! Thank You that You love me so much that You haven't answered certain prayers. You haven't allowed certain people into my life whom I really wanted, because they would have limited my growth. I know You are in complete control. There is no power greater than Yours. I believe that my steps and my stops are ordered by You. I know just as You can close doors, You will open them. So I'm keeping a good attitude. I'm moving forward in faith, knowing that You have my best interests at heart. I believe the reason You close certain doors is because You have something better in store.

Takeaway Truth

You may be discouraged because your plans have not worked out, but those closed doors were not an accident. That was God directing your steps. The reason God closed them is because He has something better in store. Thank God for your closed doors just as much as for your open doors. I believe and declare you will see the exceeding, abundant, above-and-beyond future that God has in store.

CHAPTER
19

God Is in Control of the Storm

> **Key Truth**
> God never said He would prevent
> life storms, but He did promise
> He would use every storm for
> His divine purpose.

M ost of the time we believe God is in control when everything is going our way. We're getting good breaks. Business is up. The family is happy. We know God is directing our steps. Life is good.

But having faith doesn't exempt us from difficulties. The storms of life come to every person. We get a bad medical report. A friend betrays us. Business takes a downturn. In the difficult times it's easy to think, "God, where are You? How could You let this happen to me?"

But the same God who is in control in the good times is just as in control in the tough times. God will not allow a storm unless He has a divine purpose for it. He never said He would prevent every difficulty, but God did promise He would use every difficulty.

Here's the key: God will direct the winds of the storm to blow you where He wants you to go. We see storms as being negative, but God uses the storm to move you from point A to point B. The winds may be strong, the circumstances may look bad, but if you will stay in faith, not get bitter, not start complaining, those winds will blow you to a new level of your destiny.

It may have been meant for your harm, but God knows how to shift the winds. Instead of blowing you backward, He can cause them to blow you forward where you will come out better, stronger—and that storm also will move you to a place of greater blessing and greater influence. Instead of using your faith to try to pray away every difficulty, you should use your faith to believe that when the winds stop blowing, you will be exactly where God wants you to be.

The three Hebrew teenagers Shadrach, Meshach, and Abednego were facing a huge storm. They were about to be thrown into a fiery furnace because they wouldn't bow down before the king's golden idol (Daniel 3). I'm sure they prayed for deliverance. They wanted God to do it their way, but God chose to do it another way. Sometimes God will deliver you from the fire. Other times God will make you fireproof and take you through the fire.

There are two kinds of faith. There is a delivering faith and there is a sustaining faith. Delivering faith is when God keeps you from the fire. God keeps you out of the adversity. But most of the time we need sustaining faith. Sustaining faith is when God takes you through the storm, through the difficulty, and the wind is blowing. You are filled with doubt, anxiety, fear, and bitterness. You have all these opportunities to get discouraged. But when you know that God is in control of the storm, you won't be worried. He will make you fireproof.

The same God who kept them safe in the fiery furnace has put a hedge of protection around you. Whether you realize it or not, you are fireproof. You are coming out stronger, increased, promoted, and without smelling like smoke, just like those teens.

Why? Almighty God is in control of the furnace. He is in control of the winds. God is even in control of our enemies.

Consider This

God promised the Apostle Paul that he would stand
before Caesar, yet on the way to Rome his ship was
caught in a storm so strong and huge that the crew was
certain they would all perish (Acts 27). Paul was doing
the right thing, but was caught in what seemed to be a
never-ending storm. Even so, he remained calm, believing
God would not have allowed this storm if it would keep
him from his destiny. How have you responded to life's
storms? How might you better respond?

What the Scriptures Say

But Joseph said to [his brothers who had sold him into slavery], "Don't be afraid. Am I in the place of God? You intended to harm me, but God intended it for good to accomplish what is now being done, the saving of many lives."

Genesis 50:19–20

Daniel answered, "May the king live forever! My God sent his angel, and he shut the mouths of the lions. They have not hurt me, because I was found innocent in his sight. Nor have I ever done any wrong before you, Your Majesty."

Daniel 6:21–22

Thoughts for Today

Storms make oaks take deeper roots.

George Herbert

Not until we have passed through the furnace are we made to know how much dross there is in our composition.

Charles C. Colton

We are always in the forge, or on the anvil;
by trials God is shaping us for higher things.

Henry Ward Beecher

A Prayer for Today

Father God, I am at peace today because I know You control the winds and storms of my life. They can either blow me backward, forward, sideways, up, or down. But one thing I'm confident in: Where You take me is where I'm supposed to be. You are in control in the good times as well as the tough times. The fierce winds may come, but You will shift the winds in my direction. I believe that instead of defeating me, they will promote me.

Takeaway Truth

What is your test now will soon

become your testimony. Shake off the

discouragement. Shake off the self-pity and

get ready for God to do something new.

Those winds blowing against you are about

to shift direction. They will thrust you

forward into the fullness of your destiny.

Part V:
Don't Settle for Good Enough

CHAPTER
20

Don't Settle for Good Enough

> **Key Truth**
> Good enough is not your destiny as
> a child of the Most High God.

God brought the people of Israel out of slavery in Egypt. They were headed through the wilderness toward the Promised Land, a land flowing with milk and honey. The spies came back and said, "Moses, we have never seen such a magnificent land so beautiful, luscious, green." That was the vision God had in front of them.

In the wilderness they saw God's goodness. They saw God part the Red Sea, bring water out of a rock, and rain down manna from Heaven. But do you know that was all only temporary provision? When they came to the Promised Land, all the people of Israel had to do was fight for the land. God had promised them the victory, but they were not willing to fight. They thought, "It's not worth it. It's too much trouble. Besides, those people are bigger than us, anyway."

I believe one reason they settled for less than the Promised Land is because they had seen God's favor in the wilderness. They thought, "It's not so bad out here. God takes care of us. He feeds us. He clothes us. It's good enough." They were too easily satisfied. They didn't realize everything God had done up to that point was only to sustain them until they reached their land of abundance.

Don't make the mistake of settling for "good enough." Good enough is not your destiny. You are a child of the Most High God. You have seeds of greatness on the inside. If you are to see the fullness of what God has in store, you have to have the right attitude: "I'm not letting good enough be good enough. I know I was created for greatness. I was created to excel, to live a healthy life, to overcome obstacles, to fulfill my destiny. I am not settling. I'm stretching. I'm letting go of the things that didn't work out and reaching forward to the new things God has in store."

Maybe you have lost your fire. At one time you may have known you would break an addiction, beat a sickness, or find someone to marry, but you've gone through disappointments. Your life has not worked out the way you thought it would. Now you've accepted the fact that your vision for your life will probably not happen. You've become comfortable with good enough. But God is saying to you what He said to the people of Israel: "You have dwelt long enough on this mountain."

It's time to move forward. God has new levels in front of you, new opportunities, new relationships, promotions, and breakthroughs. But you need to stir up what God put on the inside, stir up the dreams and the promises you've pushed down. God will make a way where you can't see a way. He will connect you to the right people. He will open doors no man can shut. What God spoke over your life, what He promised you in the night, what He whispered in your spirit, those hidden dreams, He will bring to pass.

My challenge to you is this: Don't settle where you are in your health, your relationships, your career, or your walk with the Lord. Keep stretching. Keep growing. Keep believing. Keep dreaming. Don't let good enough be good enough. Be determined to become everything God created you to be.

Consider This

The Scripture says, "No eye has seen, no ear has heard, no mind has imagined the amazing things God has in store for those who love the Lord." Have you settled somewhere way beneath what you know God has put in you? Have you given up on a dream or let go of a promise because it didn't happen the first time? How will you respond to God saying that it's time to move forward?

What the Scriptures Say

—◆—

When the LORD your God brings you into the land he
swore to your fathers, to Abraham, Isaac and Jacob, to
give you—a land with large, flourishing cities you did not
build, houses filled with all kinds of good things you
did not provide, wells you did not dig, and vineyards
and olive groves you did not plant . . .

Deuteronomy 6:10–11

"Enlarge the place of your tent, stretch your tent curtains
wide, do not hold back; lengthen your cords, strengthen
your stakes. For you will spread out to the right and to
the left; your descendants will dispossess nations and
settle in their desolate cities."

Isaiah 54:2–3

Thoughts for Today

—◇—

Jesus Christ opens wide the doors of the treasure house of God's promise and bids us go in and take with boldness the riches that are ours.

Corrie ten Boom

Complacency is a deadly foe of all spiritual growth.

A. W. Tozer

If you have accomplished all that you have planned for yourself, you have not planned enough.

Meggido Message

....
....
....
....
....
....
....
....
....
....
....
....
....

A Prayer for Today

Father, thank You for Your goodness, protection, provisions, and favor. You've been awesome in my life and I thank You for it. But I believe this is only temporary provision. Where You're taking me is to a land of abundance, a place like I've never experienced before. I believe that something out of the ordinary is coming my way; new levels of favor, unprecedented opportunities, or divine connections. I'm pulling up my stakes and moving forward with You.

Takeaway Truth

You may have dwelled on that same mountain long enough. It's time to pull up your stakes. Pack up your belongings. Start moving forward. Enlarge your vision. Make room in your thinking for the new thing God wants to do. Don't let your temporary provision become permanent. If you'll learn this principle of stretching and not settling, then you will see the fullness of what God has in store and make it all the way to your Promised Land.

CHAPTER
21

You Are Uncontainable

> ### *Key Truth*
> You are a child of Almighty God,
> created to grow, move forward, increase,
> and constantly break the barriers of the
> past and advance God's Kingdom.

I love the story in Acts 4, in which Peter and John prayed for people and they became well. Great miracles had taken place. They had a big service. All kinds of good things happened. But instead of being happy about it, the city leaders opposed them and ordered it to stop. They were saying in effect, "We're pushing them down to lessen their influence and contain them."

But Peter and John understood this principle. They knew: "We cannot be contained. God put this dream in our hearts, and as long as we stay in faith, nothing can shut it down." Their message was not restricted. It spread like wildfire, and we're still talking about it today.

In the same way, we cannot be contained. When God created us, He put seeds of increase on the inside. We were never made to reach one level and stop. We were created to grow, to move forward, and to increase. We should be constantly breaking the barriers of the past, taking new ground for our families and advancing God's Kingdom.

But throughout life there will always be forces trying to keep us where we are. They can't stop the progress we've made, but they'll do their best to contain us, to keep us in a box and to limit our influence.

Here's the good news: You are uncontainable. The forces in you are greater than the forces trying to contain you. If you're to become everything God has created you to be, you can't get stuck in a rut and think you've reached your limits. Keep stretching your faith, looking for new opportunities, new ideas, and new ways to expand your influence. You were made for more, to influence more, to accomplish more, to love more, to give more, and to have more. God will take you places you've never dreamed of. He will bring opportunities that give you amazing influence.

You need to dig your heels in and say, "I will not be contained by negative people, by the way I was raised, by mistakes I've made, by injustice, disappointment, or even some handicap. I am a child of the Most High God. He breathed His life into me. I have something incredible to offer. Where I am is not where I'm staying. I'm rising higher. I'm a barrier breaker. I'm taking new ground for God's Kingdom."

Nelson Mandela was put in prison because he opposed the government of apartheid. He could have thought, "I did my best, gave it my all. I guess it wasn't meant to be." Instead, Mr. Mandela knew he couldn't be contained by people, by injustice, by racism, by hatred, or even by prison walls. Twenty-seven years later, he walked out a free man. Eventually, he became president of that same country and won the Nobel Peace Prize.

What God has destined for your life will come to fulfillment. God is going to increase your influence. Rid yourself of that limited mentality and press forward in faith. God will make you a barrier breaker. God is about to thrust you into a new level of your destiny. You cannot be contained.

Consider This

When the Apostle Paul was imprisoned for spreading the Good News, his captors thought they were containing him. Paul could have become discouraged and given up. Instead, he proceeded to write much of the New Testament from a prison cell and is still profoundly influencing us today. What does it mean to you that God has made you uncontainable? What seeds of greatness are waiting to take root and flourish in your life?

....
....
....
....
....
....
....
....
....
....
....
....
....
....
....
....
....

What the Scriptures Say

Not that I have already obtained all this, or have already arrived at my goal, but I press on to take hold of that for which Christ Jesus took hold of me. Brothers and sisters, I do not consider myself yet to have taken hold of it. But one thing I do: Forgetting what is behind and straining toward what is ahead, I press on toward the goal to win the prize for which God has called me heavenward in Christ Jesus.

Philippians 3:12–14

You, dear children, are from God and have overcome them, because the one who is in you is greater than the one who is in the world.

1 John 4:4

....

....

....

....

....

....

....

....

....

....

....

....

....

Thoughts for Today

We never become truly spiritual by sitting down
and wishing to be so.

Phillip Brooks

Nothing is ever wasted in the Kingdom of God. Not one
tear, not all our pain, not the unanswered question or the
seemingly unanswered prayers. Nothing will be wasted
if we give our lives to God. And if we are willing to be
patient until the grace of God is made manifest, whether
it takes nine years or ninety, it will be worth the wait.

Author Unknown

Don't assume you have to be extraordinary to be used
by God. You don't have to have exceptional gifts, talents,
abilities, or connections. God specializes in using ordinary people whose limitations and weaknesses make
them ideal showcases for His greatness and glory.

Nancy Leigh DeMoss

....
....
....
....
....
....
....
....
....

A Prayer for Today

Father, thank You that because I am Your child,
I don't have to be contained by how I was raised, by my
education or environment, or by what I've been in the
past. I'm pressing forward and taking new ground,
stretching my faith, believing for bigger things, expecting
Your favor in unprecedented ways. Because Your face is
shining down on me right now, where I am is not where
I'm staying. I'm not getting comfortable. I'm not stuck in
a rut. If You are for me, who dares be against me?
I believe I am uncontainable.

Takeaway Truth

In the coming days, God will bring opportunities for you to increase your influence in amazing ways. Don't shrink back in fear. Don't be intimidated. You are well able. You are equipped. You are anointed. Dare to take those steps of faith. What you've seen God do in the past will pale in comparison to what God is about to do. Get ready for God's favor and blessings. You are uncontainable.

CHAPTER
22

Develop Your Pearl

> **Key Truth**
> Every irritation in our lives is
> designed to become a pearl.

You may not have realized this, but pearls—one of the most beautiful, natural, and expensive jewels—are made from irritations. Oysters feed off the bottom of the ocean, and occasionally something will become lodged on the inside of the shell and irritate the oyster. It responds by covering it with the same material used to create the shell. When fully coated, the "irritant" becomes a beautiful pearl.

In the same way, God designed every irritation in our lives to become a pearl. He allows us to be in uncomfortable situations where we're not getting our way, not being treated right, or things are not happening as fast as we would like. This pressure brings to light impurities in our character, things like pride, selfishness, being critical, or easily offended. These are traits we need to get rid of.

The irritation was never designed to frustrate you. It was designed to help you grow, to help you develop the pearl. I've learned you can't pray away every uncomfortable situation. You can't rebuke every trial. God allows difficulties to help us grow. He uses people who are hard to get along with like sandpaper to rub the rough edges off us. If we don't understand how God operates and the process He uses, then we'll go through life frustrated, wondering why God is not answering our prayers, and running from every difficulty.

The Apostle Paul said in Romans 8:18, "Our present sufferings are not worth comparing with the glory that will be revealed in us." Paul was mistreated, lied about, and persecuted. He had to put up with all kinds of unfairness, but he didn't complain. He didn't try to run from every difficult situation. He said in effect, "These hard times, these irritations, are no big deal. They're helping to develop my pearl. I know God is using them to do a work in me."

A lady who attends Lakewood Church always comes without her husband. She deals with a lot of issues at home. For years she came down front for prayer. She had this list of all the things she wanted God to fix. She didn't think she could be happy unless they all turned around. The main thing she wanted to change was her husband. Then, I saw her one day at church and she was just beaming with joy and more at peace than I had ever seen her. I thought surely everything must have worked out. But she said, "No, Joel. My husband is just the same, but you know what? I have changed. I don't let that frustrate me anymore. I don't let him keep me from enjoying my life."

What happened? She let that irritation become a pearl. When you can be happy, not because of your circumstances, but in spite of your circumstances, then something is deposited on the inside that nothing can take away.

I've learned that God is not as interested in changing my circumstances as He is in changing me. Where you are is not nearly as important as who you are. While God is changing the "where," allow Him to change the "who." He wants to bring the pearl out of you.

Consider This

The Scripture says if we're to share in Christ's glory, we must be willing to share in His sufferings. The suffering the Scripture refers to occurs when we have to say no to our flesh, when we remain calm after we don't get our way, and when we stay in faith even when life seems unfair. Our character is being developed in this way. Our pearls are being polished. What are the "irritants" in your life that God is using to become pearls?

What the Scriptures Say

Yet you, LORD, are our Father. We are the clay, you are the potter; we are all the work of your hand. . . . Does the clay say to the potter, "What are you making?"

Isaiah 64:8; 45:9

Dear friends, do not be surprised at the fiery ordeal that has come on you to test you, as though something strange were happening to you. But rejoice inasmuch as you participate in the sufferings of Christ, so that you may be overjoyed when his glory is revealed.

1 Peter 4:12–13

....
....
....
....
....
....
....
....
....
....
....
....
....
....
....

Thoughts for Today

As followers of Christ, we often suffer not because
we are out of God's will but because we are in it, not
because we lack faith but because we have faith. We suffer
not because we need to be filled with the Spirit but because
we already are. Stronger faith does not mean less suffering,
but more suffering means stronger faith. Far from calling
our faith into question, our afflictions result in our
becoming more and more like Christ Himself.

D. R. McConnell

In order to mold His children,
God sometimes has to melt them down.

Author Unknown

In adversity we usually want God to do a removing
job when He wants to do an improving job.

Author Unknown

A Prayer for Today

Father in Heaven, thank You that You don't send irritations to make my life miserable. You know there is a pearl in me waiting to be formed as I surrender my will to You. You know what I'm going through and where I am, so I must need it. I'm not fighting against it. I'm embracing the place where I am. I know You have given me the grace to be here. I thank You that You are changing me little by little, from glory to glory. I believe that my present sufferings are nothing compared to the glory that is coming.

Takeaway Truth

The Scripture says, "After you have passed the test you will receive the victor's crown of life." My challenge for you is that you pass your test. There is a victor's crown waiting for you. Your sufferings are nothing compared to the glory that is coming. If you stay moldable, pliable, and willing to change, you won't be at this same place next year. God will take every irritation and turn it into a pearl.

CHAPTER
23

Get over It

> **Key Truth**
> Get over anything holding you
> back from the amazing future
> God has in store.

Too many people go through life thinking somebody owes them something. If they didn't have a perfect childhood, they're angry at their parents. If they were laid off after many years with a company, they're upset with their bosses. Or maybe they came down with an illness. Life threw them a curve. Now, they have a chip on their shoulder and bitterness on the inside. They ask: "If God was so good, how could He let this happen to me?"

But God never promised life would be fair. He did promise that if you stay in faith, He would take what is meant for your harm and use it to your advantage. Nothing that happens to you is a surprise to God. That's why He's arranged a comeback for every setback, a vindication for every wrong, and a new beginning for every disappointment. Don't let one bad break, a divorce, or a rough childhood cause you to sour on life.

If you get over it, God will still get you to where you're supposed to be. The person who did you wrong in a relationship, the betrayal, or the divorce might have caused you pain, but if you get over it, quit reliving all the hurt, and move forward, then you'll come to the new beginning God has in store.

My message is very simple, and I offer it with respect: Get over whatever wrongs have been done to you. Don't let bitter feelings take root. Your attitude should be: "Nobody owes me anything. I am not at a disadvantage. I didn't get left out, shortchanged, passed over, or cheated. I am equipped, empowered, and anointed. All the forces of darkness cannot keep me from my destiny."

Think about the story of Job. He had a lot to get over. He lost his health, his family, and his business. If anybody had a right to have a chip on his shoulder, to be angry and bitter, it would have to be Job. He was a good man. He loved God. He was being his best. Yet his life was turned upside down.

Job could have given up on life and blamed God. Instead, right in the middle of his challenges, when he could have been bitter and sour, he looked up to the heavens and said, "Though He slay me, yet will I trust Him."

He was saying in effect, "No matter what comes my way, I'm not getting bitter, angry, offended, or carrying a chip on my shoulder. My situation may not be fair. But I know a secret. My God is still on the Throne. He will make my wrongs right. I may not like it, but I'm going to get over it and keep moving forward."

Nine months later, Job came out with twice what he had before. When you get over it, you position yourself for double. When you forgive someone who did you wrong, get ready for double. When you have a good attitude even though life has thrown you a curve, get ready for double. When you go through life being your best, even though it seems like you're at a disadvantage, get ready for double. God says to you what He said to Job, "Double is coming your way."

Double the joy. Double the peace. Double the favor.

Consider This

When we hold on to things we should let go,
refusing to forgive, remembering the worst, we only
poison our own lives. Hebrews 12 talks about a root of
bitterness. I've learned that a bitter root will always
produce bitter fruit. Bitter people don't have good relationships. They're too negative. When we're bitter, it affects
our attitudes and taints everything about us. What issue
in your life is God saying to you, "Get over it"?

....
....
....
....
....
....
....
....
....
....
....
....
....
....
....
....
....

What the Scriptures Say

"When you pass through the waters, I will be with you; and when you pass through the rivers, they will not sweep over you. When you walk through the fire, you will not be burned; the flames will not set you ablaze. For I am the LORD your God, the Holy One of Israel, your Savior . . ."

Isaiah 43:2–3

"But I tell you, love your enemies and pray for those who persecute you, that you may be children of your Father in heaven. He causes his sun to rise on the evil and the good, and sends rain on the righteous and the unrighteous."

Matthew 5:44–45

Thoughts for Today

Acrid bitterness inevitably seeps into the lives of
people who harbor grudges and suppress anger, and
bitterness is always a poison. It keeps your pain alive
instead of letting you deal with it and get beyond it.
Bitterness sentences you to relive the hurt over and over.

Lee Strobel

Forgiveness is the economy of the heart. Forgiveness saves
the expense of anger, the cost of hatred, the waste of spirits.

Hannah More

God has a big eraser.

Billy Zeoli

A Prayer for Today

Father, I recognize that You are not surprised by what was lacking or hurtful in my past or present. You know every hardship and hurt, every unfair and difficult situation I have faced and will ever face. I choose to let go of the things that are holding me back from the fantastic future You have for me. I choose to forgive others as You have forgiven me, and I ask You to cleanse any poison of bitterness out of my life. I believe that You are moving me forward and will thrust me into my destiny.

Takeaway Truth

If you learn this simple principle to get over it,

then I believe and declare no disappointment,

no bad break, and no injustice will keep you

from your destiny. God will take what's meant

for your harm and use it to your advantage.

Like Job, you will not only come out of the

difficult times, you will also come out better,

stronger, and increased, with twice the joy,

twice the peace, and twice the victory.

CHAPTER 24

Put Actions behind Your Faith

> ### Key Truth
> God is looking for people who have faith that He can see, a faith that is demonstrated.

The Scripture tells us there was a paralyzed man who asked four of his friends to carry him to a home where Jesus was teaching. When they arrived, it was so crowded they couldn't get in. I'm sure they were exhausted and could have easily given up, but instead they hoisted him up on the roof and began to take the roof tiles off. Finally, they lowered this paralyzed man into the room.

The Scripture says in Mark 2:5, "When Jesus saw their faith." God is looking for people who have faith that He can see. Not a faith that He can just hear, not a faith that just believes, but a faith that is visible, a faith that is demonstrated. There were other people in the room who didn't get well. Other people had the same opportunity. The difference was this man put actions behind his belief, and he received his healing.

Are you doing something to show God you're serious about your dreams coming to pass? God is not moved by our needs. He's concerned about our needs, but God is moved by our faith. When God sees you doing what you can to get well, when He sees you getting to work a little earlier because you want that promotion, when He sees you bypass the cookie jar because you've been believing to lose weight—that is when extraordinary things will happen.

A man I know felt called into the ministry. He took a step of faith by renting the small auditorium of a high school for his first service. He invited his friends and neighbors to come, and he spread the word through the town's newspaper, but not a soul showed up. My friend was alone onstage. The only other person was a technician in the sound booth. He was so disheartened, but just as he was about to give up something rose up on the inside, a holy determination.

"I'm not going home a failure. I've prepared my message," he thought. "I've taken this step of faith, so I'm giving it my all."

Without one person in the auditorium seats he preached as if the place was packed, giving it his very best. At the end he even invited people to come forward and receive Christ. As he finished his invitation, a side door opened and a janitor walked down to the front and said, "I want to accept Christ." A few seconds later, the sound technician joined them, saying, "I want to make a commitment to Christ."

The young minister went home that night not feeling like a failure at all. Instead, he knew the hand of God was on his life. That was a turning point. Door after door opened to him after that. Today, he has a church with thousands of people in the congregation.

Can God see your faith? Are you doing anything to demonstrate your trust? The action you take does not have to be something big. It could be just a small step that activates God's favor. But when you take time to honor God, He is moved by your faith. Your faith is opening the door for the extraordinary.

Consider This

―◈―

"When Jesus saw their faith." Here's my question for you. Do you have a faith that God can see? Are you doing something out of the ordinary to show God you believe Him?

....
....
....
....
....
....
....
....
....
....
....
....
....
....
....
....
....
....
....
....
....

What the Scriptures Say

. . . do you want evidence that faith without deeds
is useless? Was not our father Abraham considered
righteous for what he did when he offered his son Isaac
on the altar? You see that his faith and his actions were
working together, and his faith was made complete by
what he did. And the scripture was fulfilled that says,
"Abraham believed God, and it was credited to him as
righteousness," and he was called God's friend. You see
that a person is considered righteous by what they
do and not by faith alone.

James 2:20–24

As he was going into a village, ten men who had leprosy
met him. They stood at a distance and called out in a
loud voice, "Jesus, Master, have pity on us!" When he saw
them, he said, "Go, show yourselves to the priests."
And as they went, they were cleansed.

Luke 17:12–14, emphasis mine

....
....
....
....
....
....
....
....

Thoughts for Today

God, I pray Thee, light the idle sticks of my life and may I burn for Thee. Consume my life, my God, for it is Thine. I seek not a long life, but a full one, like You, Lord Jesus.

Jim Elliot

It is impossible, indeed, to separate works from faith, just as it is impossible to separate heat and light from fire.

Martin Luther

It is better to fail in an attempt to exercise faith than to let it lie dormant and fruitless. God never belittles those who attempt to follow Him, but He does chasten those who refuse to attempt anything for Him.

Kent Hughes

A Prayer for Today

Father, I want to live the full and abundant life that You have promised me. I'm going to show You I'm serious about fulfilling my destiny by taking a step of faith to put actions behind what I'm believing. I've waited and waited for everything to fall into place, thinking once it does then I'll stretch, and then I'll make a move, but it's time to take action. I want my faith to activate Your favor and goodness. I believe that I will find power to do what I couldn't do before and that extraordinary things are going to happen. I am expecting my miracle.

Takeaway Truth

Have a faith that God can see. Put actions behind what you believe. It's not enough to just pray, not enough to just believe. Take it one step further and demonstrate your faith. You may not see how your dream could ever work out, but as you take steps of faith, you'll see God begin to open new doors. You'll have the strength to do what you could not do. You'll see His favor in unusual ways.

CHAPTER
25

God Will Finish What He Started

> ### *Key Truth*
> When the Creator of the universe placed a dream in your heart, He also set a completion date to bring it to pass.

The moment God put a dream in your heart, the moment the promise took root, God not only started it, but He set a completion date. God is called the Author and the Finisher of our Faith. He wouldn't have given you the dream, the promise wouldn't have come alive, if He didn't already have a plan to bring it to pass.

Maybe at one time you believed you could do something great. You had a big dream. You believed you could start that business. Believed that you'd get healthy again. Believed that you'd fall in love and get married. But it's been so long. You tried and it didn't work out. Now, the "I'll never accomplish . . ." lies are playing in your mind.

"No," God is saying, "it's not over. I have the final say. I set the completion date." It doesn't matter how long it's been or how impossible it looks. If you will stay in faith and not talk yourself out of it, it's just a matter of time before it comes to pass.

You have to have a new perspective. The Creator of the universe has already set that completion date. Just because it hasn't happened yet doesn't mean it's not going to happen. God has already lined up the right people, the right breaks, the right answers. Everything you need is already in your future. Now, you've got to shake off the doubt, shake off the discouragement. Whether it's been a year or fifty years, what God promised you He still has every intention of bringing it to pass.

In the Scripture, it says that the Holy Spirit revealed to a man named Simeon that "he would not die before he had seen the Lord's Messiah" (Luke 2:26). You can imagine how far out that promise seemed. As time went by, and Simeon didn't see any sign of the Messiah, I'm sure the negative thoughts came: "You heard God wrong. It's been too long. It's never going to happen." Nevertheless, Simeon awakened every morning believing, expecting, and knowing that it would happen, and one day it did. The promise came to a dramatic fulfillment and Simeon declared, "My eyes have seen Your salvation!"

God is saying to you what He said to Simeon: "You need to get ready. I am going to finish what I started. No one and nothing can stop Me from fulfilling My promises. I will complete your incompletions, even the secret petitions of your heart."

Life will try to push you down, steal your dreams, and talk you into settling for mediocrity. But I want you to have this new attitude and believe that whatever God started in your life, He will finish. Here's the real question: Will you keep believing even though it looks impossible? Will you stay in faith, even though every voice tells you that it's not happening?

Here's how the Scripture puts it: "Being confident of this, that he who began a good work in you will carry it on to completion" (Philippians 1:6). God remembers the dreams He placed in your heart. Get your fire back. Get your passion back. Things have shifted in your favor. God is going to finish what He started.

Consider This

The Scripture says that for years Rachel desired to have a baby but could not conceive. After she had given up on her dream, it says that "God remembered Rachel; he listened to her and enabled her to conceive" (Genesis 30:22). It doesn't say that Rachel remembered God. This is how much God wants you to fulfill your destiny. So what are the incompletions in your life that you need to stay in faith about?

....

....

....

....

....

....

....

....

....

....

....

....

....

....

....

What the Scriptures Say

"Praise be to the LORD, who has given rest to his people Israel just as he promised. Not one word has failed of all the good promises he gave through his servant Moses."

1 Kings 8:56

But it was because the LORD loved you and kept the oath he swore to your ancestors that he brought you out with a mighty hand and redeemed you from the land of slavery, from the power of Pharaoh king of Egypt. Know therefore that the LORD your God is God; he is the faithful God, keeping his covenant of love to a thousand generations of those who love him and keep his commandments.

Deuteronomy 7:8–9

Thoughts for Today

Wait on God and He will work, but don't wait in
spiritual sulks because you cannot see an inch in front of
you! Are we detached enough from our spiritual hysterics
to wait on God? To wait is not to sit with folded hands,
but to learn to do what we are told.

Oswald Chambers

God never made a promise that was too good to be true.

D. L. Moody

God's most striking victories arise out of
the graves of apparent defeat.

Author Unknown

. . . .
. . . .
. . . .
. . . .
. . . .
. . . .
. . . .
. . . .
. . . .
. . . .
. . . .
. . . .
. . . .

A Prayer for Today

Father in Heaven, I thank You that You will bring to completion the good work You began in me. You promised to complete my incompletions. So, Lord, I want to thank You that the fulfillment of my dreams is on the way, even the secret petitions of my heart. You spoke the worlds into existence, and You have me in the palm of Your hand. I believe You will make sure I complete what You put me here to do.

Takeaway Truth

The moment God put a dream in your heart, the moment the promise took root, God not only started it, but He set a completion date. God will bring your dreams to pass. Now do your part and break out of anything holding you back. Pray God-sized prayers. Don't settle for good enough. *Yes* is in your future. Move forward in faith, and your seeds of greatness will take root. You will go beyond your barriers and become everything God created you to be, and you will have everything He intended for you to have.

STAY**CONNECTED,** BE**BLESSED.**

From thoughtful articles to powerful blogs, podcasts and more, JoelOsteen.com is full of inspirations that will give you encouragement and confidence in your daily life.

AVAILABLE ON JOELOSTEEN.COM

today's**W RD**

This daily devotional from Joel and Victoria will help you grow in your relationship with the Lord and equip you to be everything God intends you to be.

Joel Osteen
STREAMING

Miss a broadcast? Watch Joel Osteen on demand, and see Joel LIVE on Sundays.

Joel Osteen
PODCAST

Put Joel in your pocket! The podcast is a great way to listen to Joel where you want, when you want.

Plus, connect with us on your favorite sites.

facebook.com/JoelOsteen

twitter.com/JoelOsteen

Thanks for helping us make a difference in the lives of millions around the world.